GENDER INCLUSIVE
GAME DESIGN

Expanding the Market

GENDER INCLUSIVE GAME DESIGN

Expanding the Market

Sheri Graner Ray

CHARLES RIVER MEDIA, INC.
Hingham, Massachusetts

Publisher: Jenifer Niles
Production: Paw Print Media
Cover Design: The Printed Image

CHARLES RIVER MEDIA, INC.
10 Downer Avenue
Hingham, Massachusetts 02043
781-740-0400
781-740-8816 (FAX)
info@charlesriver.com
www.charlesriver.com

This book is printed on acid-free paper.

Sheri Graner Ray. *Gender Inclusive Game Design: Expanding the Market.*
ISBN: 1-58450-239-8

Library of Congress Cataloging-in-Publication Data

Graner Ray, Sheri.
  Gender inclusive game design : expanding the market / Sheri
Graner Ray.—1st ed.
    p. cm.
  ISBN 1-58450-239-8
  1. Computer games—Design—Social aspects. 2. Computers and women.
I. Title.
  QA76.76.C672G76 2003
  794.8'1526—dc22
                              2003016397

Printed in the United States of America
05 7 6 5 4 3 2

CHARLES RIVER MEDIA titles are available for site license or bulk purchase by institutions, user groups, corporations, etc. For additional information, please contact the Special Sales Department at 781-740-0400.

With love to Tim,
who has listened to me spout this for so long,
and yet still stays married to me!

CONTENTS

Acknowledgments   xi

Introduction   xiii
    References   xvii

1 Females and Machines   1
    1.1 Early Socialization with Computers   3
    1.2 Commercialization of Behavior Patterns   4
    1.3 Gender Differences in Attitudes
        Toward Technology   6
    1.4 Gender and Software Design   6
    1.5 Application of Concepts   8
    References   15

2 Evolution of Female Characters in
Computer Games   17
    2.1 Early Character Representations   18
    2.2 Challenging the 'Damsel in Distress' Concept   21
    2.3 The Emergence of the Female Protagonist   25
    2.4 The Rise of the Female Avatar   27
    2.5 The Female Image—
        Contrasts and Compromises   28
    References   36

3 Conflict and Conflict Resolution Styles
in Game Design   37
    3.1 Conflict Subjects   38
    3.2 Conflict as a Definition of "Game" 40
    3.3 Gender Differences in Conflict Resolution   43

3.4   Direct vs. Indirect Competition   45
3.5   Application of Concept   46
      References   50

4   Stimulation and Entertainment   51
    4.1   The Male Stimulation Response   52
    4.2   The Female Stimulation Response   54
    4.3   Emotional Stimulation   56
    4.4   Tactile Stimulation   57
    4.5   Application of Concepts   60
          References   65

5   Learning and Communications Styles
    in Computer Game Development   67
    5.1   Spatial Relations   68
    5.2   Risk Taking   70
    5.3   Electronic Communication Styles   72
    5.4   Application of Concepts   74
          References   81

6   Reward and Gameplay   83
    6.1   Scores and Levels   84
    6.2   Response to Error   84
    6.3   Cooperative Play   85
    6.4   Application of Concepts   88
          References   91

7   Avatar Selection   93
    7.1   The Evolution of Avatars   94
    7.2   The Pyramid of Power   95
    7.3   Token Character Classes   100
    7.4   Representation of Avatars   102
    7.5   Application of Concepts   105
          References   107

8   Puzzle Games   109
    8.1   Definition of "Puzzle"   110

8.2   Puzzles and the Nontraditional Game Audience   111
8.3   Application of Concepts   113
        References   116

9   Online and Wireless Games   117
9.1   The Flexibility of Online Games   118
9.2   Reward Systems in Online Games   119
9.3   Story in Online Game Design   119
9.4   Improving the Online Game Design   121
9.5   Interfaces and Tutorials in Online Games   122
9.6   Females and Player vs. Player Games   123
9.7   Wireless Entertainment   124
        References   128

10   The Design Document—A Case Study   129
10.1   Parts of a Design Document   130
10.2   Sample Design Document and Revisions   131
10.3   Product Overview   132
10.4   Gameplay Overview   135
10.5   Technology Overview   143
        References   145

11   Women in the Game Industry Workplace   147
11.1   Why Does This Industry Need Women?   148
11.2   Examine the Company   149
11.3   Finding the Female Candidates   152
11.4   Supporting the Female Employee   155
11.5   Sexual Harassment   157
11.6   Benefits for the Whole   161
        References   163

12   Influential Women in
      Computer Game Development   165
12.1   Anne Westfall   166
12.2   Roberta Williams   167
12.3   Brenda Laurel   168
12.4   Laura Fryer   170

12.5 Jane Jenson   171
12.6 Ellen Guon Beeman   173
12.7 Nicky Robinson   175
        References   177

13 But What If the Player Is Female?   179
        References   184

Index   185

ACKNOWLEDGMENTS

Special thanks to: The Women in Game Development committee of the IGDA and their mailing list for their ideas, input, and support; Ellen Guon Beeman for her support and access to her amazing contact list; Paula Marks, Ph.D. at St. Edwards University for her support and encouragement; Midori Sushi and La Madeline Café for letting me sit for hours and write; and my family and my grandmother, Vera Donnelly, who turned 100 in 2002 and has never once stopped believing in me.

INTRODUCTION

There are many debates over exactly when the computer game revolution began and what titles started that revolution. But it can safely be said that *Pong* was the first commercially successful home entertainment computer product. It was marketed as fun for the entire family, and the advertisements showed a family enjoying the game. It was a dramatic success and was *the* gift to have under the tree that holiday season. After *Pong* came more titles, such as *Centipede* and *Pac-Man*. They were all billed as fun for the whole family.

About this time the game industry's concept of the market began to change. With the arrival of such titles as *Donkey Kong* and *Dragon's Lair,* the idea of 'fun for the whole family' began to fade away. By the early 1990s, the market had firmly established itself as a 'males, ages 13–25' domain, and publishers began to churn out title after title aimed squarely at that market. As the competition increased, the companies began to try to outdo each other with their machismo slants in order to capture a larger share of this tightly defined market.

Then in 1995, Patricia Flanagan, marketing director for American Laser Games, Inc., recognized that a large segment of the gaming population was going untapped. That market was female. She persuaded American Laser Games to open a division called Her Interactive, with the goal of producing computer entertainment titles specifically for girls ages 10 and older. After much research work and many focus groups, they approached publishers with their designs and demographics in hand. To their surprise, instead of the interest they expected, they were turned away and simply told, "Girls don't play computer games." But Her Interactive was certain of their market, so the company decided to self-publish their titles, and *McKenzie & Co.* was released in 1996. This small title, which was self-published and marketed from Albuquerque, New Mexico, went on to sell 80,000 units. Yet the industry continued to believe that 'girls don't play computer games.' Then one year later, Mattel® released a title that would have a lasting effect on the computer game industry. *Barbie Fashion Designer* hit the shelves and sold over 600,000 units in its very first year [Rolling97]. These numbers certainly got the big industry publishers to take note. The industry's attitude began to change from "*Why* should we make games for girls?" to "*How* should we make games for girls?"

Very close on the heels of *Barbie Fashion Designer*, another company opened its doors with the goal of targeting the girls market. Purple Moon, with its funding from Paul Allen's group and with Brenda Laurel at its head, began to produce a line of titles based upon a spunky female character named Rocket. Rocket's adventures were well received and soon found shelf space right alongside *Barbie™* titles in major retail stores across the country.

The industry began to scramble to get titles out for the female market. Sega released its *Cosmo Virtual Makeover* line, The Learning Company followed with its *American Girl* series, and even Electronic Arts got in on the action with *Michelle Kwan Figure Skating*. However, while the industry could finally see the potential in the market, they had no established marketing channels into it, and the traditional channels just didn't seem to work.

The numbers for the other girls' titles did not come close to reaching the blockbuster numbers *Barbie Fashion Designer* was pulling in, so the publishers began to cut their production costs. As the quality of the games dropped, so did the sales figures. Finally, the only titles that sold well were those whose licenses had enough power to overcome the channel problem: *Mary Kate and Ashley* (Activision), *Nancy Drew* (Her Interactive), and to a lesser extent, *Rocket* (Purple Moon).

Then in 1997, citing failing sales numbers, Purple Moon shut its doors. Shortly thereafter, Mattel closed down its interactive division and began to sublet out production on their *Barbie* titles. Regardless of the actual reasons, these events were seen by the industry as the failure of the girls game movement, and so they turned their backs on the female market. *Barbie* was a fluke, they declared—a title that continued to sell only because of the strength of its license.

By the early 2000s, there were very few alternative titles on the market for females. In almost a backlash against the female market, games began to show up that seemed to go out of their way to exclude the female players. Titles like *DOA Xtreme Volleyball,* where girls clad in thong-style bikinis bounce, jiggle, and giggle their way through games of beach volleyball, appeared on the shelves, almost as if to say: "See, we *told* you girls didn't play games."

This attitude, which persists to this day, is short-sighted and ultimately detrimental to the game industry itself. As the industry has matured, rather than expanding its audience for games, it has actually narrowed its focus and has stopped considering family games, such as *Pong,* in favor of the extremely limited markets of *DAO Extreme Volleyball.* And yet, the industry argues, sales numbers continue to climb, so much so that revenues from computer games sales now outreach movie receipts [Holland02]. This might suggest that everything is fine. However, developers need to think about the future growth of this industry and what the market *could* be. If a title today started from an audience base 50% larger than the traditional audience, and then continued to grow from there, the result would be astonishing. But, is that possible? Does the audience exist?

The audience *is* there, and they are more tech savvy than they were in the late 1990s. Today, females make up 52% of the Internet users in this country. Research shows that 70% of the casual online gamers are female [Meretzky02]. Somehow, though, these numbers start to drop when the traditional game market is mentioned; suddenly, only one in 10 console gamers is female [IGN02].

So somewhere, somehow, a disconnect is occurring that is keeping females away from traditional computer games. If it were strictly a technology issue, then we wouldn't see the percentage of female users of the Internet, casual games, and chat services continuing to rise. If we, as designers, want to bridge this gap and reach this untapped market, then we need to take a good look at the content we are providing for our games. Many times, it's not just that there isn't anything out there that might attract a female player; but often, what is out there contains content that actually serves as a barrier to women, preventing them from accessing and enjoying it.

The question then becomes how do we design titles that reach out beyond the traditional market and yet still keep the genre integrity? Is it even possible? We found that putting games into pink boxes only really worked for Mattel, and there are only so many *Cosmopolitan* licenses to go around. So, it's going to take more than window dressing or name brands to attract female gamers. It's going to take designers that are willing to look at different conflict resolution styles and different learning styles. It's going to take artists that are willing to rethink how they present avatars. It's going to take design teams that keep the broad market in mind from the very first lines of the design document, and it's going to take development houses that are willing to examine their hiring practices and make sure they are an option for potential female industry candidates. In short, it's going to take an industry that is willing to step back and look at their titles, and ask themselves, "But what if the player is female?"

These and other issues are the topics we are going to look at in this book. We will attempt to understand the differences between males and females, and then look at various ways to apply these differences to the traditional genres that make up the contemporary computer game industry. By expanding our design knowledge to include this new knowledge, we will not only expand our market, but we will design better games.

REFERENCES

[Holland02] Holland, Angus, "How the Other Half Plays," *The Age* (May 26, 2002), available online at *http://www.theage.com.au/articles/2002/05/25/1022243279705.html.*

[IGN02] IGN, "Nintendo Speaks Out," (October 31, 2002), available online at *http://www.cube.ign.com/articles/376/376063p1.html.*

[Meretzky02] Meretzky, Steve, interview with author; August 16, 2002.

[Rolling97] "ROLLING eye, eye WONDER," *Eye Weekly* (October 23, 1997), available online at *http://www.eye.net/eye/issue/issue_10.23.97/rolling/rolleyewonder23.html.*

CHAPTER 1

FEMALES AND MACHINES

In the mid-1990s, when the question of how to make games for a broader market came up, many developers thought the answer would be easy. Just ask people what they want in a game, and then make that game. Seemed like a logical approach. One particular developer set out to do just that and worked out an arrangement with the local computer game store to do some in-store surveys. She put together her questions, got a clipboard, and showed up at the store on a Saturday morning, ready to solve the problem.

Unfortunately, at the end of several days of this, she found that rather than finding an answer, she was left with no definite direction in which to go. Overall, the men she talked to seemed to know exactly what they wanted, be it war games, strategy games, car games, or sports games. But the women she talked to left her baffled. When they were asked, "What would interest you in a computer game?" the answer they gave was: "I work on one of those machines all day. Why would I want to turn it on when I get home?"

This was a puzzling answer to what seemed, at first, to be a straightforward question. It was a nonanswer. These women weren't only uninterested in computer games—they were uninterested in the machines, completely.

At first, this didn't make sense. If a woman worked in a television station all day, certainly she would still turn on the TV when she got home. People in the film industry are some of the biggest movie fans around, and women in the newspaper or publishing industry still read in their spare time; so an overexposure to the hardware didn't make sense as a reason. It also didn't make sense that a collection of electronic components could be gender-biased simply by virtue of its existence. Why, then, were women so loathe to turn on a computer at home?

1.1   EARLY SOCIALIZATION WITH COMPUTERS

The answer begins with the way male and female attitudes toward machines are developed at very early ages. Studies show that children begin to sort out what society expects of their gender at the age of two. By the time they are seven years old, those roles are firmly established, and the child is functioning comfortably within them [Williams93]. These roles are established through both positive and negative reinforcement. When a boy is chided for picking up his sister's purse, this reinforces the idea that 'purses are for girls.' When a girl is praised for staying clean when her brothers get dirty, 'girls stay clean' is positively reinforced [Nielsen90].

THE COMPUTER AS A 'MALE' OBJECT

Many researchers believe that the concept of the computer as a 'male' object is reinforced in children at a very early age. Boys are more frequently given machine-type toys—including computers. They are encouraged to experiment with these machines and are more likely to receive formal computer training and/or attend computer camp. Girls, on the other hand, are often given software that is productivity- or education-oriented, but this software does not necessarily directly educate them in the computer's technology. They receive little formal training and are rarely sent to computer camps.

This means that instead of "Teach Yourself Basic Programming" software, which their brothers might receive, girls are given "Learn to Type" [Fasick92]. Based on feedback from my lectures on this subject, it also very common for girls to be given a 'hand-me-down' machine, while their fathers/brothers get bigger, faster, new machines. The message conveyed is that the girls are not 'worthy' of the newest and best in computer equipment, but the males in the family are.

With the wide access to computers in schools today, it would seem that girls would have equal access, and this early socialization could be overcome. However, this has not proven to be the case. While there are certainly more computers in schools, access to them is not always gender-equitable. In the majority of schools, computers are located in the math or science classrooms, areas that are historically hostile to girls. Also, studies done by Brenda Laurel, formerly of Purple Moon, backed up observations made at Her Interactive. When the number of machines is not equal to the number of students, boys will dominate them by physically 'crowding out' the girls [Hanscome95].

1.2   COMMERCIALIZATION OF BEHAVIOR PATTERNS

These behavior patterns and stereotypes extend into the commercial market and all the way to the retail stores. In an attempt to find out what women were being offered, a casual survey was performed by the author in the mid-1990s of the titles on the shelves at various software stores in Albuquerque, New Mexico.

To determine what was being marketed toward women, the survey began by listing titles that did not have hypersexualized women featured on their covers. It was immediately apparent these titles were not entertainment software. Rather, they were productivity titles, such as *Mavis Beacon Teaches Typing* or *Better Homes and Gardens Healthy Cooking.*

To explore this further, one of the clerks was asked what titles were available for women. He stopped and thought about it for a moment. Then he pointed to the shelf that contained productivity titles, such as home budget software and recipe organizers. A number of other software stores were also visited, and the clerks were asked the same question. In every store, the counter help was male. And in every store, the response was the same: a puzzled look, and then direction to the shelf containing productivity software. Not only were there no entertainment titles aimed at the female market, but the entertainment titles that *were* available were not offered when clerks were asked to suggest software for females.

The survey seemed to suggest that the reason women were not turning on their computers at home was because they had not been encouraged by the software publishing industry to see the computer as an entertainment (fun) medium for them, as women. They had not been given any entertainment titles that were designed with their entertainment criteria in mind, and they were not encouraged to try the titles that were available. Software that was marketed to women was specifically productivity or self-improvement related. Because of this, women have been trained to see the computer as a productivity tool, much like an adding machine, and no one would think about using an adding machine for entertainment at home.

This denial of entertainment technology has far-reaching implications. It is one of the reasons why women, who represent a majority of the general population, comprise a minority when it comes to technology careers. A conversation with any male programmer in the game industry will probably reveal that he is there because he played computer games as a kid. He loved the games, but always thought, "I can make one even better!" He will talk about building .WAD files for *Doom* and sharing them with friends, or even of building simple games of his own. This led him to look into the computer game industry and computer programming in general as a possible career. But a girl's chances for a career in programming are slim if her only exposure to the industry has been hours spent with *Mavis Beacon Teaches Typing.*

In short, we cannot expect women to excel in technology tomorrow if we don't encourage girls to have fun with technology today.

1.3   GENDER DIFFERENCES IN ATTITUDES TOWARD TECHNOLOGY

Sociologist Sherry Turkle showed that males and females approach the computer with different attitudes [Turkle88]. According to her research, males see machines as a challenge, something to be mastered, overcome, and be measured against. They are risk takers, and they demonstrate this by eagerly trying new techniques and approaches. According to Turkle, this is an attempt to dominate the machine, and is actually an extension of their desire for personal, physical power.

Turkle describes the female approach to computers as 'soft,' meaning a female user's attitude toward the machine is tactile, artistic, and communicative. She will approach the machine as a tool, and attempt to work with it in a cooperative manner. So, rather than dominate the machine, she attempts to work *with* it to achieve her goals. For her, the machine is a collaborative partner and an extension of her power of communication [Turkle88].

1.4   GENDER AND SOFTWARE DESIGN

This concept of computers as 'male' can be seen even in the design of software titles. Huff and Cooper conducted a study in 1987 to examine the issue of gender bias in software design [Huff87]. In this study, software programmers were instructed to design education software for seventh-grade children. Some of the programmers were told they were designing for boys, some were told they were designing for girls, and a third group of programmers was simply told they were designing for seventh-grade children, with no indication of gender.

The programs produced by the programmers designing for 'boys' and 'children' were very similar in theme, look, and feel. They were primarily game-based and required more hand/eye coordination, quicker reflexes, and had more action on the screen.

However, the software designed by the programmers designing for 'girls' were very different in tone, nature, and make-up. The programs designed for girls were strictly learning tools with little to no entertainment factor.

The assumption here is that when the designers were not given a specific gender, they assumed they were designing for males. The second thing it tells us is that they assumed that girls would not be interested in a 'game' style of learning, or that they would not be capable of performing the actions required in a game. This is an interesting point. Instructors have long known that both males and females learn better, and enjoy the learning experience more, when the information is presented in a 'play' format.

The difference in gender-based software design was shown again in work done by Yasmin Kafi at the Massachusetts Institute of Technology (MIT) Media Lab in 1993 [Kafi93]. In her study, she challenged same-sex groups of fourth graders to design a game that would teach fractions. The games designed by the girls and the games designed by boys were very different and defined along gender lines.

First, the themes of the games were quite different. The boys' games were distinctly goal oriented. They focused on 'getting something,' such as a lost or stolen item to be retrieved through a hunt or an exploration adventure. Most of their games closely resembled many of the commercial console titles they were already familiar with.

In contrast, the girls' games were activity based. The object of the game was the activity itself. In one case, the player had to land a plane at an airport. In another, the player had to navigate their way around a spider web. There were no objects to be recovered or won. Instead, gameplay centered on the activity and how well the player could perform it.

Probably the most dramatic difference between the games was seen in the consequences for failure. In the boys' games, failure was met with punishment that was usually violent, and which resulted in the player's 'death.' In one game, the player was 'kicked to the moon'; and in another, the player was 'sent frying to the under-world.' In all cases, the resulting death ended the game, and the player had to start over.

The girls' games dealt with failure in a completely different fashion. The consequence for a wrong move in the girls' games was usually passive feedback. Something was withheld from the player, or the player's progress was blocked. In no case was the player forced to start over from the beginning of the game. There was an element of forgiveness and an opportunity for the player to correct their error and try again.

1.5   APPLICATION OF CONCEPTS

This seems to be almost a 'chicken or the egg' problem. Women, on average, don't view computers as entertainment, so they do not purchase games for themselves. Therefore, there really isn't a market for games that are geared toward women, because women aren't playing the games, because they don't see computers as entertaining, because there isn't software . . . and around and around it goes.

How do we break this cycle, then? We break it by understanding what technologies women are comfortable with, what technologies they are interested in, and applying those features to the games we are currently building. It has become apparent that the 'killer app' we expected would suddenly attract a *huge* female audience is not going to occur. Instead, women are coming to discover computer games slowly and steadily. And the titles that are bringing them in are the ones that take female entertainment criteria into consideration when they are designed.

At the very beginning of the design process, the developers need to consider what the player motivation is for playing and completing the game. Often, this point is overlooked; the designers already have in mind what type of game they are building. Whether it be a flight sim, first person shooter (FPS), or a driving game, the motivation already has a historical precedent. It is easy to simply do what has been done before and rush right into building the game. However, in order to reach a bigger market share, it is important to look past these traditional models and explore something better.

ACTIVITY-BASED DESIGN

Traditional motivations run the gamut from 'find the magic dingus' to 'beat your opponent' in driving/fighting/flying competition. Very few of the titles, with the exception of *SimCity*-type games, are actually activity based. At first glance, they do not seem to lend themselves to activity-based motivation. For instance, the 'quest' is the heart and soul of Fantasy Role-Playing games (FRPs). There is usually an item to be recovered, an evil enemy to be slain, and a world to be saved. The idea of making it 'activity' based seems out of the question. However, with careful planning, activity-centered play models can be part of the overall design.

The titles in the original *Ultima* PC game series were the quintessential RPGs. They were epic in scale, had many items that had to be recovered in order to 'save the world,' and there was an evil enemy to be slain. However, there were also activities within the world that had no bearing on the outcome of the overall quest. For instance, the player could gather wheat, grind it into flour, mix the flour into dough, and bake the dough in the oven to produce bread. None of this had any bearing on the title's main story line. Nonetheless, it was an amazingly popular activity within the game. So popular, in fact, that these activities were the seed idea for many of the guilds and activities that serve as the basis for the economy in *Ultima Online*, which, at the time of this writing, is still going strong.

There are other ways to incorporate activity-based goals within a title. One of the most common ways is to allow the players to customize their avatars. While this may bring to mind 'Barbie-esque' titles, avatar customization is enjoyed by males as well as females. Recently on a fan-run bulletin board for *Asheron's Call*, a Massively Multiplayer Online RPG (MMORPG), the players were discussing trying a new online game in which the player's avatar was a spaceship. One player mentioned that in the game, you do not ever see yourself. Another (male) player immediately responded that if he couldn't see himself, choose what he looked like, and choose what he was wearing, as well as see the other players, then he doubted he'd enjoy the game. Another member suggested that perhaps the game would allow him to customize his ship so it would better represent him. This pleased the unhappy player, and he agreed that, if that were the case, he would try the game.

There are many other ways to expand the player's motivation through activity-based play. In a 3D world, perhaps the player could be allowed to experiment with the terrain features or to design a new location within the game. This could be used in Real-Time Strategy (RTS) games where the terrain is incidental to gameplay. Or perhaps the player could be allowed to customize his base of operations—something that may not affect the game's outcome, but which would provide alternative play patterns.

It is important to note that these types of activities, which have little to no effect on the main story or final outcome of the game, are often trivialized. They are usually the first things cut from a design in order to save time or to implement other 'action' features. However, to do so could be shortsighted; we would be removing those things that could help to expand a title's audience beyond its traditional market base.

THE MACHINE AS THE 'FOE'— HIDDEN GAME COMPONENTS

While developing the concepts for the motivation for the player, it is also important to consider the player's approach to the machine. Females are more comfortable working *with* machines, rather than attempting to master them. This means that to increase the comfort level for female players, the interface needs to be extremely intuitive. The machine should not be portrayed as 'the foe'; in fact, it should be transparent to the software.

A classic example of a machine being a 'foe' to be overcome can be seen in the current wave of fighting games. A staple of these games are the 'secret moves' a player must find by experimenting with different key strokes. Hiding important game components within the technology (machine) inherently pits the player against the technology, making the hardware something the player must overcome.

In a recent discussion on the Women in Game Development mailing list (*http://www.igda.org/women*), members were discussing titles that had recently been released. Though there was much excitement over these new titles, there was also disappointment on playing them. One of the women mentioned that she had purchased a popular fighting game for her PlayStation® 2 (PS2). She considered herself pretty good; but one day, her boyfriend challenged her to play. He promptly bested her. She was disappointed, particularly when she noticed he was using all sorts of moves she had never seen before. There was nothing about those moves in the manual, so she asked him where he had learned them. He replied that he had learned these moves just by pushing the buttons a lot. This made her quite unhappy with the game, so much so that she ceased to play it. The machine as a 'foe' became a barrier to her enjoyment.

Thus, to avoid creating these barriers for a percentage of the potential audience, the game mechanics should be intuitive and easy to learn. The fundamentals of play should not be 'hidden' within the technology, as this requires the player to 'fight' the technology in order to enjoy the game. In some genres, such as fighting games, hidden moves are traditional. But designers need to develop ways to allow players to discover the hidden moves within the context of the game as well as through trial and error with the keypad. Perhaps the player could be presented with puzzles or questions, and the correct answer will reveal a new move. Or maybe the player could hunt for clues to secret moves by clicking on various areas of the screen. Providing the information about secret moves on Web sites, in manuals, or in other publications is also a possibility, but it is not the most optimal method for several reasons. First, it breaks the continuity of the game as well as its suspension of belief. Second (and probably most destructive to the game), it encourages the player to continually leave the game flow. Each time a player leaves the game, there is a chance the player will not return. As designers, we want our players to remain in the game as long as possible. Also, it is possible that they will not be able to find the information they are looking for, resulting in a barrier to gameplay.

CONSEQUENCES AS BARRIERS TO GAMEPLAY

Consequences for actions can also be barriers for many players. Designers need to carefully consider how they structure the response for an incorrect action. The traditional way to deal with a 'wrong' action is to 'kill' the player and require him to start over. While this is the easiest to design, it is not the most comfortable outcome for female players. Therefore, it is important to consider other methods of dealing with incorrect actions throughout the design phase of the project.

In the title *Vampire Diaries*™, a story-based RPG released by Her Interactive in 1996, the design team identified 'fatality' locations, those areas of the game where the player was given the opportunity to make a choice that could result in death. At these locations, the player's character and game information were saved automatically without the player's knowledge. If a fatal choice was made, the player was shown a video clip of the vampire attacking, and was then given a screen that said, "Try Again?" If this option was selected, the player would find themselves back in the game at the point where they entered the location with the fatal choice. The scenario could be tried again, or the player could simply leave the area and try another route altogether, and there would be no punishment (e.g., loss of equipment, experience, or other vital statistics) for 'dying.'

But the question then comes up, should there be punishment for 'wrong' decisions in a game at all? This is a design question that has caused many lively discussions at game development conferences. There certainly should be some sort of consequences for a wrong decision in gameplay. Without challenges and consequences, games would be rather boring. It's the *form* that the consequence takes that may determine how large an audience the title draws.

For solutions to this problem, designers need to reach past the usual answers of 'die and start over' or 'revert to saved game' to deal with the problem of consequences. Ways must be considered to 'forgive' a player for his or her actions, rather than punish them. In this way, the player would not be 'killed'; their progress in the game would only be delayed. For example, in a flight sim, say the player is shot down during a mission. Instead of starting over at the beginning, the player could be given the opportunity to try again in a new plane, or perhaps allowed to attempt an alternate mission. All of this would be done without the loss of any character points or equipment. If the player were to be given a set number of planes for their attempts, and they still managed to botch each mission, then perhaps the player could be returned to the previous, 'easier' mission to try again. This would not 'kill' them, but it would, instead, simply block progression in the game until the mission was mastered.

Myst is a very good example of a game that employs non-lethal consequences for incorrect answers. In no place in the game *Myst* is the player 'killed.' If the player does not solve a puzzle correctly, they are simply prevented from progressing in the plot line. This forgiveness for error is only one of the design features that made *Myst* one of the best selling titles of all time.

REFERENCES

[Fasick92] Adele M. Fasick, *What Research Tells Us About Children's Use of Information Media*, CLJ, February 1992.

[Hanscome95] Hanscome, Barbara, "Beyond the Chrome and Sizzle," *Game Developer Magazine*, February 1995.

[Huff87] Huff, C. and J. Cooper, "Sex Bias in Education Software: The Effect of Designers' Stereotypes on the Software They Design," *Journal of Applied Social Psychology* (1987), Vol. 17, no. 6.

[Kafi93] Kafi, Y. B., "Minds in Play: Computer Game Design as a Context for Children's Learning," Doctoral Dissertation, Harvard Graduate School of Education, Cambridge, MA, 1993.

[Nielsen90] Nielsen, Joyce McCarl, *Sex and Gender in Society, Perspective on Stratification*, Waveland Press, Inc., IL, 1990.

[Turkle88] Turkle, S., "Computational Reticence: Why Women Fear the Intimate Machine," *Technology and Women's Voices: Keeping in Touch.* Ed. C. Kramarae, London: Routledge, 1988.

[Turkle98] Turkle, S., "Computational Reticence; Why Women Fear the Intimate Machine," in C. Kramare (ed.), *Technology and Women's Voices,* New York: Routledge & Kegan Paul.

[Williams93] Williams, Ogletree, Woodburn, and Raffeld, "Gender Roles, Computer Attitudes, and Dyadic Computer Interaction Performance in College Students," *Sex Roles* (1993), Vol. 29, nos. 7, 8.

CHAPTER 2

EVOLUTION OF FEMALE CHARACTERS IN COMPUTER GAMES

The very earliest computer/electronic games didn't have gender representation, mostly due to the limitations of the graphics technology. Early games were more representative than literal. In *Pong*, the square pixel on the screen represented a ball, and the two vertical lines represented paddles; while in *Asteroids*, the small triangle in the center of the screen represented a spaceship, and the jagged balls hurtling toward it were asteroids. The main character in *Pac-Man* was a yellow ball; the only indication of gender was the "*Man*" in the game's name.

2.1 EARLY CHARACTER REPRESENTATIONS

It wasn't until the appearance of a small yellow ball with a pink bow on top of it that the industry saw the birth of gender in a video game. This little, yellow, pink-bowed ball is still probably one of the most famous and most recognizable computer game characters—*Ms. Pac-Man*.

MS. PAC-MAN

Released in 1981, *Ms. Pac-Man* was originally intended to be a sequel to the already popular arcade hit, *Pac-Man*. But its publisher, Midway, wanted to design more than just a sequel. They wanted a title that would reach beyond the established market to a new market: female players. With the graphics limitations of the time, they decided the best way to make the main character female was to put a bow on her head and line her mouth with red to give the appearance of lips. They also changed the screen colors to pastels and gave the antagonists 'cute' nicknames, such as "Sue," which was supposedly after one of the designer's sister [DeMaria,Wilson02].

Along with these changes, there were several technological advances in the game, such as two to four mazes that changed instead of just one, and prizes that moved around the maze.

FROGGER

The same year that *Ms. Pac-Man* was released, another female character hopped into the picture. In the immensely popular game *Frogger*, the player could pick up a female frog on his back and carry her to the safety of his lily pad. Again, the graphics were limited. The way the designers indicated that the frog was female was to color her pink. If the player made it all the way to the lily pad with the pink 'girl' frog on his back, the player won bonus points.

It is interesting to note that at the time of *Frogger's* release, arcades were primarily a male domain. If girls were present at all, they were standing at their boyfriends' backs, watching them play, much like the female frog clinging to Frogger's back as he moved through traffic. (You can see an image of the female frog at *http://www.members. aol.com/chrissalo/frogger.htm.*)

DONKEY KONG

In 1984, another groundbreaking title was released—*Donkey Kong*™. In *Donkey Kong,* the player controlled a small, roundish carpenter named Jumpman (who later changed his occupation to plumber and his name to Mario) as he tried to rescue his girlfriend, Pauline, from a huge gorilla. (You can see early shots of *Donkey Kong* at *http://www.classicgaming.com/rotw/dk.shtml.*)

It is interesting to note the difference in the promotional art and the art that actually appeared in the game. At this point in time, raster graphics had become advanced enough to allow the artists to distinguish between male and female, but only in the most rudimentary ways. Pauline's dress and long hair marked her as female, whereas Jumpman's mustache denoted him as male. Also, for the first time, a female character had a speaking role. Pauline repeatedly said "Help!" in the game.

In the promotional flyer, however, Pauline is depicted in great detail, resembling Fay Wray's Ann Darrow in *King Kong*. Trapped against a wall by a big gorilla, she swoons in her stiletto heels, while one strap of her dress has slipped provocatively off her shoulder. Because this type of detail was not possible in the game, the designers used their promotional artwork, which also appeared on the game arcade cabinet, to help direct the players' imaginations.

DRAGON'S LAIR

A second notable title was released in 1984 by Cinematronics. *Dragon's Lair* was the first arcade game to utilize laser disc technology. Finally, the designers were able to use hand-drawn cel animation, rather than computer-generated animation. This made for gameplay that was as beautiful and detailed as any cartoon on television.

The premise of *Dragon's Lair* was typical: the princess Daphne has been kidnapped by an evil wizard and must be rescued by the valiant knight, Dirk the Daring. The player controls Dirk as he journeys through the dark castle, trying to find Daphne.

With the amazing amount of detail in the animation, it was no longer a matter of simply differentiating between male and female characters. The artists for *Dragon's Lair* could develop characters with depth and personality. Dirk was presented in typical medieval dress: tunic, hose, boots, and coif. For Daphne, however, instead of wearing medieval-style clothing like her would-be rescuer, they put her in a black, low-cut, one-piece outfit that resembled lingerie or a leotard, and on her feet were stiletto-heel shoes. This type of clothing was certainly not suitable for an easy escape; it reinforced the idea that Daphne was a helpless (if alluring) female who needed rescuing. (You can see images of Daphane at *http://www.dragons-lair-project.com/community/artwork/default.asp.*)

2.2 CHALLENGING THE 'DAMSEL IN DISTRESS' CONCEPT

Up until the 1980s, female characters in computer games were, for the most part, damsels in distress, and the protagonists in the games were male. Notable exceptions to this were the classic text adventure, *Leather Goddesses of Phobos*, and games such as *Gauntlet* and *Carmen San Diego*.

LEATHER GODDESSES OF PHOBOS

One notable exception to the 'damsel in distress' theme was Infocom's *Leather Goddesses of Phobos*. Released in 1983, it was one of the classic text adventures designed by the legendary Steve Meretzky. In the opening sequence of the game, the player is sitting in a bar in Upper Sandusky, Ohio. Suddenly, 'nature calls,' and the player is given a choice of entering either the men's or the women's restroom. The player's choice will determine how the game treats the player's character. If the player choose the men's room, then his companion for the rest of the game is a character named "Tiffany." If the player chooses the women's room, then her companion is "Trent." In either case, the slant of the gameplay follows suit. This was the first time a computer game took the gender of the player's character into consideration and changed the context of the game accordingly. The ironic part of this is that *Leather Goddesses of Phobos* was designed to be an 'adult' game filled with sexual innuendoes that could have been rife with the familiar stereotypes and clichés. Instead, Meretzky delivered a risqué, funny, and now classic game title.

■ **STEVE MERETZKY ON** *LEATHER GODDESSES OF PHOBOS.*

Because we were making a game based on sexual innuendo, we knew that the content would have to be different for males than females. I didn't want to be so heavy handed as to require the player to click a button in the beginning of the game, so we put it in the game, in the form of the restroom choice.

At that time, the majority of the game audience was less than five percent female. The audience for Infocom games was roughly 25%–30% female. So we knew we had a female audience and designed the title accordingly.

The games today are becoming more and more restricted in their subject matter. Accordingly, the audience is also being limited. The casual game market doesn't receive much attention or respect by the industry. Until the industry begins to broaden its view and take the casual gamer into consideration, they will not realize the market potential that is out there [Meretzky02].

GAUNTLET

Another exception to the 'damsel in distress' depiction was 1985's immensely popular arcade game, *Gauntlet. Gauntlet* was a four-person arcade game in which the players worked together to battle their way through a dungeon.

Gauntlet suffered from the same raster graphics issues that *Donkey Kong* did, so simply establishing the character's gender was a problem. However, the artists once again used their promotional/cabinet art to spark the players' imaginations. The promotional art featured the male warrior and the female Valkyrie characters. They are dressed in an interesting combination of fantasy and techno garb, wearing what appears to be armor, but carrying shields that appear to be circuit boards. An image of this is available at *http://www. basementarcade.com/arcade/guant/*.

In the original version of the title, there were four preset characters: the Warrior, the Mage, the Elf, and the Valkyrie. The Warrior was the strongest character and could take the most damage, but he was slow. The Elf was the quickest character, but could take the least damage. The Mage had powerful magical spells, but was not good at hand-to-hand combat. The Valkyrie, however, was a well-balanced character, somewhere between the Elf and the Warrior in her effectiveness. Therefore, she was often the choice character to play. This type of balanced female character would not show up again in computer games until much later.

 It is interesting that in the home version of the game, there were two cheat codes. One allowed the player to play the game with the Valkyrie character nude, except for censor bars. The other cheat code allowed the player to play as a totally nude Valkyrie.

CARMEN SAN DIEGO

Another ground-breaking, 'edu-tainment' title was released in 1985 by Broderbund, and it is still popular today: *Where in the World is Carmen San Diego?* This game was notable not only because it was an enormously popular education/entertainment title, but because it was one of the first hit titles to have a female antagonist. Carmen San Diego is a smart, crafty thief who steals the fine treasures of the world and leaves clues behind. The players decipher the clues in order to figure out where she has taken the treasures. While the players would retrieve the stolen treasures, Carmen San Diego would always manage to slip from their grasps.

LEGEND OF ZELDA

1986 saw the first appearance of one of the longest running game series, the *Legend of Zelda*. In this series, Zelda is a princess who, in order to save her kingdom, has hidden pieces of a valuable treasure around her kingdom. She then calls in Link, a knight, to drive off the Dark Lord who threatens her kingdom. The series primarily focuses on Link and his adventures at trying to save the kingdom. Thus, *Zelda* is a bit of a twist on the 'rescue the princess' theme; but here the princess recognizes she has to be saved and selects the person who will do it.

MANIAC MANSION

In 1987, another breakthrough title was released. Lucas Film's *Maniac Mansion* was a title that had many firsts in it. Because it featured the new 'point-and-click' interface, it was the first adventure game that did not require the player to type in their actions. It was also the first game to feature a side-scrolling screen.*

Maniac Mansion allowed you to choose what people you wanted on your team in order to accomplish your mission. Two of the choices were female: Razor, the rock-and-roll singer; and Wendy, the up-and-coming novelist. Each character had unique talents that, when brought to the team, could make solving the puzzles easier. However, the plot was a familiar one. Dave's girlfriend, Sandy, has been kidnapped by a mad scientist, and it's up to the gang to save

---

* A side-scrolling game is a two-dimensional game where the avatar stays roughly in the center of the screen but the landscape scrolls by to keep the avatar's actions centered.

her). You can see images of the girls, and boys, from *Maniac Mansion* at *http://members.fortunecity.com/harang/describe.html.*

2.3   THE EMERGENCE OF THE FEMALE PROTAGONIST

Although *King's Quest* series of games began in 1984 with the release of its first title, *King's Quest I, Quest for the Crown*, it wasn't until 1988 that the series (and the home computer game industry) saw its first female protagonist.

KING'S QUEST

King's Quest IV, Rosella's Peril features the princess Rosella, who is looking for a magical fruit that will cure her dying father. Through this quest, she must work her way through various myths and legends, such as Pandora's box and the Odyssey mythos of the three witches who all share one eye. Rosella is a smart character for whom gender is not an issue. She is the princess who saves her father. You can see an image of Rosella on the game's cover art at *http://www.mobygames.com/game/covers/gameCoverId,16927/gameId,129/.*

PRINCE OF PERSIA

In 1989, another title was released that would go on to have a major influence in computer game design. That title was *Prince of Persia*. A major leap forward in side-scrolling action games, the main character leapt, ran, swung, and climbed his way through a complicated system of tunnels and traps. This realistic action would go on to influence adventure/action games for the next generation.

It was also a leap forward in graphics capability as well. The problems of the raster graphics had been left behind, and designers were now able to develop animations that were nearly on a par with commercial television cartoons. However, the reason the Prince was going through all this leaping, running, and swinging was already a cliché motivation: he was trying to rescue his princess. You can see the princess in the clutches of the evil Grand Vizier, Jaffar at *http://www.mobygames.com/game/covers/gameCoverId,383/gameId,196/*.

DUNGEON MASTER

The year 1989 also saw an improvement in 3D adventure games. *Dungeon Master*, developed and published by FTL, Inc., gave the players a first-person viewpoint in a 3D world. Another innovation was the ability of the players to control their actions through the mouse, rather than typing in commands, in order to move down corridors and into rooms where monsters waited.

Although the game had a first-person viewpoint, the avatar was not one character, but a group of characters. At the beginning of the game, the player is presented with a list of 24 potential adventurers and then selects four from that list. Of the 24 offered characters, eight are female. While the representations are not equal, the female characters are varied in their appearance, and they appear in each of the major character classes. The list of champions and their accompanying images is available at *http://dmweb.free.fr/DMChampions.htm*.

EYE OF THE BEHOLDER

This ability to choose your party of adventures had become a standard feature in action/adventure and role-playing games. In 1990, Westwood Studio released *Eye of the Beholder*, published by SSI. This was the first title in a successful trilogy of titles, all based on the Dungeons and Dragons® role-playing system. It, too, featured female characters of various types and character classes.

2.4   THE RISE OF THE FEMALE AVATAR

In 1991, a game arrived that started an entire new genre of computer and arcade games. It also allowed you to pick the gender of your avatar. *Street Fighter II*, by Capcom (the sequel to the much lesser known Str*eet Fighter I*), was a smash hit in the arcades, on home PCs, and game consoles as well.

STREET FIGHTER II

Street Fighter II provided players with a choice of seven characters, one of which was female: Chun Li. Granted, she was dressed provocatively, but no more so than her male counterparts. She was a well-balanced character and, in the hands of a skillful player, was as likely to win as the male characters.

ULTIMA VII PART TWO, THE SERPENT ISLE

Origin Systems released a sequel to the *Ultima* series in 1992 called *Ultima VII Part Two, The Serpent Isle*. While it didn't take place in the familiar world of Britannia, it did include all of the avatar's party members from *Ultima VII, The Black Gate*. However, there was one major change. Players could chose their avatar's gender and race. This was a first in computer games. The models the artists used for the female avatars were female athletes, and the armor the they wore was feminine, but not hypersexual. Overall, they were good representations of both gender and race.

KING'S QUEST, THE PRINCELESS BRIDE

In 1994, Sierra released another in the *King's Quest* series: *King's Quest VII, the Princeless Bride*. In this episode of the *King's Quest* saga, Rosella and her mother, Queen Valanice, set off to find Rosella a suitable husband. Through misadventure, they wind up on two separate paths, each 'chapter' of the story involving one character or the other. Thus, this game featured not one, but two female protagonists, something which still stands as unique.

PHANTASMAGORIA

Roberta Williams went on to produce the hit *Phantasmagoria,* which shipped in 1995. Comprising eight discs, it was a huge game and the prime example of an interactive movie or novel. This title took a detour in graphics technology. Rather than using animations, the game used footage of live actors shot against a blue-screen and then composited into a computer-generated background.

The story of *Phantasmagoria* is set on the Eastern seaboard. A young couple, Adrienne and Don, have just purchased and moved into an old mansion. They don't know it has a terrible, evil past. The evil in the place possesses her husband, and it is up to Adrienne to solve the mystery of the old mansion. Adrienne is an attractive, average woman—someone you might expect to see in the grocery store. Her clothing is simple and nonprovocative. And, in a theme Roberta Williams does well, we are presented with a princess who is out to save her prince and her home. You can see images of Adrienne (along with some commentary) at *http://www.justadventure.com/ reviews/Phantasmagoria/Phantasmagoria_Review.shtm.*

2.5   THE FEMALE IMAGE— CONTRASTS AND COMPROMISES

As we look back through the history of games, we find that (with the exceptions previously noted) there seems to be two ways game designers deal with female representation in games. The first way is by depicting the female as a sexual object. The female's sexual characteristics are exaggerated and emphasized. Even though she might have other outstanding traits, such as strength or courage, there is still an over-exaggeration of the female primary sexual traits and an emphasis on sexual receptivity.

The second way designers approach feminine representation is to depict the female as an object to be retrieved or rescued. Of course, this isn't limited to the game industry, by any means. Entertainment has been filled with "rescue the princess" imagery ever since the first story was told. Unfortunately, in the case of computer games, the repetition of this theme may have had an off-putting effect on female players. Also, the idea of 'rescue the princess' has been done so often that it has simply become cliché. Even *Dungeon*, a magazine published by Wizards of the Coast and dedicated solely to role-playing game scenarios, will not accept modules built on this theme.

Designers need to consider this when building story lines for a game. Rescuing the princess was fine for *Donkey Kong* in 1988; but today, it is simply not enough. Fresh ideas and new concepts are needed, and these innovative themes are at the heart of the truly classic games.

During the production of the classic, multi-award winning *Ultima* series of PC games, Richard Garriott continually pushed his teams to develop ideas that went beyond the cliché. He wanted to move beyond 'rescuing the princess' or 'retrieving the golden goose.'

According to Lisa Smith, designer on *Ultima VII Part Two, the Serpent Isle* team, "That was probably one of the toughest parts of design. It would have been so easy to concentrate on the 'cool' technology and just fall back to an old 'avatar as messenger boy' plot line. But we knew we wanted more than that. We wanted cool technology

and a really interesting motivation. I think we did just that"
[Smith02].

DUKE NUKEM 3D

1996 brought another block-buster hit to the game industry: *Duke Nukem 3D*. *Duke Nukem 3D* was the third title in the series. The first two were side-scrolling games*; but this title took the Duke into a 3D world.

The premise of the game was simple: aliens had invaded Earth and were abducting the (scantily clad) women. At one point, as the main character rushes to save the world, he finds himself in a strip club. There, he can flash cash at a girl on the stage, say "Shake it, baby," and the girl then exposes her breasts for the player (see Figure 2.1).

FIGURE 2.1   "Shake it, baby," from *Duke Nukem 3D*. © 2003.
Reprinted with permission from 3D Realms Entertainment.

This is an interesting variation on the 'save the princess' theme, which implies royalty, class, and even virginity. The women that Duke Nukem is out to save are strippers, and sometimes the women don't survive being 'rescued' at all.

BARBIE FASHION DESIGNER

In 1996, an unlikely female protagonist appeared on the computer scene. Barbie™ made her debut with Mattel's *Barbie Fashion Designer*. Love her or hate her, there is no question she had a major influence on the computer game industry. With sales figures topping a million units, she showed the game industry that, without a doubt, girls *do* play computer games.

Based on the Barbie fashion doll, the figure of Barbie is a faithful adaptation of that toy, right down to her unrealistic bustline, tiny waist, and slim hips. It allows girls to design and color clothing for Barbie, and then watch as Barbie models their creations on the runway.

And while *Barbie Fashion Designer* is most noted for its amazing sales record, its technological and design advances should not be overlooked. *Barbie Fashion Designer* came with a patented paper that could be run through the player's printer. The program then turned the player's screen designs into actual outfits the player could print out on the paper and actually put on their Barbie doll. This was an amazing idea. It allowed an integration between real-life play patterns and computer play patterns [Durchin00]. This strategy of 'bridging the gap' between the real and virtual worlds is part of what makes the Barbie titles so successful.

TOMB RAIDER

Today, there is one title that has managed to step beyond the "save the princess" scenario. In 1996, Eidos released a title that would star the most famous of all female protagonists in computer games to date: *Tomb Raider's* Lara Croft.

Lara Croft has been called a "female Indiana Jones, without the hat" [Davis02]. Like Indiana Jones, she runs, fights, shoots, climbs, crawls, and swims to beat the bad guys. And like the Valkyrie from *Gauntlet*, she is a well-balanced character that male players don't mind having as their avatar. Lara Croft isn't a princess that needs saving. She is the princess who saves herself.

This break from cliché is one factor that has resulted in making the game a runaway sensation. *Tomb Raider* is one of the top-selling games and one of the most successful licenses to come out of the game industry. Multiple sequels to the original *Tomb Raider* have been spawned, including action figures, books, untold numbers of fan Web sites, and even movies featuring Angelina Jolie. Figure 2.2 shows an image of the ubiquitous Lara Croft.

FIGURE 2.2   *Tomb Raider's* Lara Croft. © 1996. Reprinted with permission from Eidos Interactive *Tomb Raider,* (1996).

However, as well as she succeeds in breaking the 'rescue the princess' barrier, Lara still fails in one other area. Even though graphics limitations are a thing of the past, and artists have a great deal of leeway in developing beautiful graphics and animations, they chose to give Lara an unrealistically large bustline, a waist smaller than her head, and a very well-rounded derriere. So, while she is well-balanced in gameplay, she is still a hypersexualized female caricature that is, essentially, 'eye candy' for male players.

This depiction of Lara was carried into the other media in which she has appeared. In a television commercial for the cable TV channel G4, Lara was shown laying on a beach, playfully buried in the sand by her companion (see: *http://www.ugo.com/channels/games/features/g4/commercials.asp*). Even when on her back and covered in the sand, her very large bustline stood straight up like two large missiles. This depiction was toned down some in the *Tomb Raiders* movie. In the movie, Lara, played by Angelina Jolie, wears clothing that is attractive and very form fitting, but does seem to be correct for the type of work she is doing at the time. By the release of the second movie, *Tomb Raider, Cradle of Life*, she has even traded in her trademark hot pants and strapped down guns for khaki safari pants and more reasonable holsters.

However, while Hollywood has tempered the Lara Croft image some, the games industry seems to want to keep her hypersexualized. The box for *Tomb Raider, Angel of Darkness* features Lara Croft on the cover. She is dressed in a black midriff and short-shorts, and wears her strapped-down holsters. The interesting part about the box cover is that her bustline is embossed so that it is raised in bas relief. The customer can actually run their fingers over the cover and 'feel' Lara's breasts.

THE LONGEST JOURNEY

In 1999, another female character arrived in an RPG world that gave the gaming audience a character that was the opposite of Lara Croft. *The Longest Journey,* released in 1999 by Funcom, brought April Ryan to the forefront. The title, named "Adventure Game of the Year" by Gamespy.com, is graphically beautiful and mentally challenging. The game's main character, April Ryan, is certainly female; and, while she is attractive, she is normal in her proportions, clothing, and demeanor. The plot line of the game is standard RPG fare. The protagonist sets upon a journey to save two worlds. She does so through puzzle solving as well as action. During this time, she keeps a journal, which the player may access. In it, she reveals herself to be a strong character, but one that is distinctly female in her feelings and attitudes. Her voice-overs contain hints of self doubt and fear, as well as determination. Over all, April Ryan is a 'female' female character.

NO ONE LIVES FOREVER

In 2000, another game featuring a female protagonist captured Game of the Year honors—this time from *Computer Games* magazine. This title, *No One Lives Forever: The Operative,* produced by Monolith Productions, is an FPS set in the 1960s. It features Cate Archer, a young, beautiful operative who holds the distinction of being the first female operative to be employed by the English government. Cate is a well-presented character: she has to deal with the bad guys she is assigned to shoot, as well as the hints of sexual discrimination from within her own organization. But she handles adversity and manages to throw in clever retorts/comebacks to the put-downs from her boss. Unfortunately, Cate is depicted wearing a skin-tight cat suit with a plunging neckline. While perhaps fitting for the time the game is set in, it does stand out sharply against the business suits and casual dress of her male companions. It is interesting to note that in the sequel, *No One Lives Forever: A Spy In H.A.R.M's Way*, this was addressed, and Cate is featured wearing a short-skirted business suit, which is much more in line with the other characters in the game.

Since 1996, the game industry has seen a plethora of Lara Croft clones. She has become the new cliché. Overly buxom women dressed in skin-tight clothes and wielding large weaponry can be seen on box covers in every computer game store. Some have sold well, but most have disappeared without a trace. To be successful, designers are going to have to reach beyond the cliché motivations and hypersexualized stereotypes to find that next truly original idea that can make their title a blockbuster.

REFERENCES

[DeMaria,Wilson02] DeMaria, Rusel and Johnny L. Wilson, *High Score! The Illustrated History of Electronic Games*, McGraw-Hill/Osbourne, Berkley, CA, 2002.

[Durchin00], Durchin, Jesyca, "Girls Software Introduction/Keys to Creating Great Girl Software," Game Developers' Conference, International Game Developers Association, San Jose, CA, March 2000.

[Dungeon02] Dungeon Submission Guidelines, Your Complete Guide to AD&D Adventure Design, November 8, 2000, available online at *http://www.paizopublishing.com/writersguidelines/dungeon_writer_guidelines.pdf.*

[Davis02] Davis, Keddy, "The Evolution of Lara Croft," *Games Domain*, February 2003, available online at *http://www.gamesdomain.com/gdreview/action/lara.html.*

[Meretzky02] Meretzky, Steve, interview with Sheri Graner Ray; August 16, 2002.

[Smith02] Smith, Lisa, interview with Sheri Graner Ray; June 1, 2002.

CHAPTER 3

CONFLICT AND CONFLICT RESOLUTION STYLES IN GAME DESIGN

A t the heart of virtually all traditional computer games is a conflict situation. The 'bad guys' want you dead. The 'enemy' wants
to take your land. The 'monsters' have taken control of your castle
dungeon. The 'other guy' wants to get to the finish line before you.
In all of these cases, there is a conflict of interest or direct competition for resources that needs to be resolved. Each game has a different approach to resolving these conflicts and competitions.

This theme is the basis of virtually all traditional genres. However,
it can take different forms. Before a designer attempts to develop a
game that reaches beyond the traditional market, they must look at
the currently popular genres and identify the common conflict situations on which these games are based.

3.1   CONFLICT SUBJECTS

Probably the most common conflict situation presented to players is
the conflict over territory, and it is presented in various forms. The
genre that almost exclusively has at its heart the theme of conflict
over territory is the RTS game. While there are many different scenarios, RTSs are ultimately about control of territory. This territory
might take the form of geographic terrain, such as a continent or a
particular moon. Or, it can be transient territory, such as the space
ship in *StarCraft*. The object for the struggle can even be a fictional
version of Earth, such as appears in *Age of Empires*.

The scenarios might be varied, but they all revolve around some
aspect of territorial control: regaining control over a previously lost
area, gaining control of an unowned area, or defending territory that
is threatened by enemies. To handle the conflict, players move their
troops into the most advantageous position, and then either advance
and engage the enemy or defend against the enemy's approach. The

situation is resolved when either the opponent or the player has gained control of the disputed territory.

Another genre that extensively uses the concept of conflict over territory is the FPS. For example, id Software released the widely successful game *Wolfenstein 3D* in 1992. The precursor to *Doom*, it was a groundbreaking title that changed the face of computer gaming.

In *Wolfenstein 3D*, the player has been captured while trying to steal battle plans from castle Wolfenstein. The mission is to escape from the Nazis, secure control of the castle, and retrieve the plans so the Allies can win WWII. The territory in conflict is the castle, and the only method available for the player to achieve their goal is to kill the Nazis by shooting them with a variety of weapons. The conflict is resolved when one side eliminates the other by killing them.

Conflicts over territory are also seen in classic/space combat flight sims. In the *Wing Commander* series, the player is involved in a war with an alien race that wants to conquer the group of planets called the Terran Federation. Earth, the home planet of the player's character, is one of the planets in the Terran Federation. In order to prevent the takeover by hostile aliens, the player engages in space battles. The conflict is resolved when either the player or the aliens are killed.

Territorial control isn't the only source for conflict. Power and money are also commonly used as a basis for conflict within a game. While they traditionally employ disputes over territory, flight sims can also involve conflicts over power and money. This can be seen in *Strike Commander*, in which the player is an F-16 fighter pilot who is a member of a maverick group of privateers. The object of the game is to gain control of the trade routes and maximize profits by eliminating rival factions. Depending on the particular mission, this is accomplished by either engaging in dog fights with the enemy or by flying bombing runs that result in the elimination of enemy resources. The conflict is resolved when the opposition is forcibly eliminated through the use of weaponry.

The conflict over money and power is a staple in role-playing games. In *Diablo*, the monster, Diablo, wants control of a city that has 'wronged' it. To do this, it has possessed the king's son, and has taken control of the dungeons and catacombs under the city. To return control of the city to the rightful kind, the player must rescue the son from the demon. As the players move deeper into the dungeon, they must defeat an increasing number of minions. In doing so, the player gains money, treasure, and weapons from the slain enemies that can be sold in the town for spells, elixirs, and better weapons/armor. The final confrontation of the game occurs at the deepest level of the dungeon. There, the player confronts Diablo and battles with it to drive it from the body of the prince and from the realm forever. When Diablo is eliminated, power is returned to the king. The player's motivation during the game comprises rewards in the form of increased wealth and power—better weapons/armor, better spells, and more gold.

3.2   Conflict as a Definition of "Game"

This concept of conflict as a basis for a game is so deeply entrenched that for the majority of players, it actually defines the term "game." In 1998, a production team known for its RTS-style games was asked to develop a prototype for a new computer game. The game was a nontraditional title that involved cooperative play and constructive advancement. At one point, a portion of the game in which the players could customize their avatars was being described to the team.

One of the developers asked the producer, "How does this help you win?" The producer explained that it didn't actually help the player win. In fact, the customizations would not even really reflect on the gameplay at all, other than as strictly cosmetic additions. Furthermore, this title didn't actually have a 'winner' at all; there were no levels to attain or any sort of score. The developer stopped, thought for a moment, and then said with resolve, "Then it is not a game."

Today, many developers find themselves in this trap, confining their creative processes to the traditional definition of "game." This is not unusual. The traditional definition is deeply engrained in our culture, and holds that a game is an activity in which a player overcomes a conflict situation to achieve a goal within a specified requirement. This is declared a 'win,' sometimes also described as a 'zero-sum' outcome.

Zero-sum is a mathematical concept that states what one side gains, the other side will lose in equal measure. The amount lost or won is counted, and a winner and loser are declared. RTS games are a good example of this concept. In an RTS, the player 'gains' territory that the opponent 'loses.' By the game's end, the one that has gained the most territory is declared the winner, and the one that has lost the most territory is declared the loser. This can also be seen in RPG titles: the player gains treasure and the opponent loses it. Each of these, then, is zero-sum.

The clearly defined winner and loser concept is so pervasive that, for the majority of people, it defines the word "game." In 1999, the same producer who was developing the previously mentioned non-traditional title was invited to participate on a panel at the Southwest Interactive Expo in Austin, Texas. The topic was computer/video games, and she was asked to be on the panel to represent games for the female audience. Before the discussion began, the moderator brought the panelists together to brief them on what she wanted the panel to highlight, and to give them the list of questions she would ask. The producer quickly recognized that the moderator's questions and overview presumed that all games were zero-sum, and resulted in a win/lose outcome. The producer pointed out that this was not the case and cited examples like *The Sims* or childhood games like Ring Around the Rosey.

The moderator was stopped short by this idea. After a brief discussion, it became clear that the moderator had never considered a game to be anything other than zero-sum and was not prepared to deal with the issues brought up by alternative concepts of what a "game" might be. Finally, the moderator told the panelists that for the purpose of their panel presentation that day, *The Sims* and games like it would not be mentioned.

It is important to note that not only has the concept of zero-sum come to be the traditionally accepted definition of "game" within our culture, that it is also the type of outcome that is most comfortable for male players. Research has shown that in the general population, males will choose to resolve conflict in a confrontational manner that results in a zero-sum outcome: I win, you lose. This desire for confrontational interaction manifests itself in games as direct competition [Lewis98].

Direct competition means that players can act directly upon their opponent to affect the opponent's performance. For instance, in a basketball game, the guard may attempt to knock away the ball as the forward tries to make a basket, thus directly interfering with the opponent's ability to score. In a flight sim, the player shoots at the opponent in order to eliminate him/her and gain control of the territory. Similarly, car racing is a directly competitive sport by this definition; the players maneuver their vehicles to directly prevent competitors from crossing the finish line first.

3.3   GENDER DIFFERENCES IN CONFLICT RESOLUTION

The male desire for direct competition and binary outcome is reflected in basic human societal patterns. Patriarchal societies arise when there is pressure for area resources, such as water, land, or food.

This can be dramatically seen in the East African culture of the Hadza. In the spring, during the time of plentiful resources, the culture is matriarchal in nature. Women provide much of the society's guidance, and conflicts are worked out through compromise and negotiation [Sanday81]. However, in the summer and fall when the harsh weather has made resources scarce, the culture assumes a patriarchal and more aggressive character. The males take a more active role in the decision-making process for the society. Conflicts are worked out through battle, as the males aggressively seek to protect their resources. In other words, when faced with a threat to the tribe's survival, the male reaction is to approach the problem as a direct confrontation with a decisive win-or-lose result [Sanday81].

While this method of resolving conflict is particularly male, research shows that women will typically choose to approach a conflict situation in a very different manner. When faced with a conflict, females will choose negotiation, diplomacy, and compromise over direct confrontation [Sanday81].

A look at some of the earliest human societies might enlighten us on how this came about. In the ancient hunter/gatherer societies, females of childbearing age spent the majority of their time either pregnant or lactating. This was due not only to the lack of birth control, but also to the fact that the human female cycled on a 28-day basis—there were frequent opportunities to become pregnant. With pregnancy and nursing as a way of life, the idea of physical confrontation with the possibility of injury or loss of resources was abhorrent. Physical confrontation could result in incapacitation or even death, and her death would also result in the death of any children that depended upon her. Therefore, it was in everyone's best interest to choose a diplomatic, and thus safer route [Neilsen90]. Compromise also helped in another way. If a resolution could be reached that was acceptable to all parties, then the possibility of conflict in the future was minimized, reducing even further the risk of direct and possibly dangerous confrontation.

While this might be ancient history, these concepts still hold true today and were observed firsthand during focus group testing of a game in 1997 by Her Interactive (Albuquerque, NM). During testing of one of their early titles, they quickly discovered that if a mixed-gender group was brought in to test, it was vital to make sure there were as many machines as there were participants. If not, the males in the group would dominate the machines by physically 'crowding out' the girls. Occasionally some of the girls would attempt to negotiate for time on the machine, but this was not often successful. So, the majority of the girls ended up standing by and watching the boys play. When asked about this, their responses were generally, "it wasn't worth fighting over." They had chosen to avoid the conflict, rather than deal with a head-to-head confrontation over the machine.

It was also discovered that if an all-female group was brought in, and there were not enough machines for all of the participants, the girls easily shared the machines. Sometimes, even when there were enough machines for everyone, they would still share—preferring to work together for a positive outcome. These findings were corroborated by a study done in 1993 by the University of British Columbia's computer science department and funded by Electronic Arts. In that study, the researchers found that if the boys were in front of the machine, the girls would not attempt to take control [Hanscome95]. Interestingly, the Albuquerque group also found that if an all-male group was brought in, and there were not enough machines for each participant, fights inevitably broke out for control of the machines. And, sometimes, if there were enough machines, there were occasional fights over control of the machines that the boys perceived as 'the best.'

The desire to avoid physical conflicts should not be construed to mean that females do not like competition. Nothing could be farther from the truth. Females can be every bit as fiercely competitive as males. One need only watch the finals of female equestrian competition or a girls' soccer game to see that. However, this competition takes a slightly different form in that it is usually either team oriented or it is indirect competition. And this difference can also be clearly seen in the area of computer games.

3.4   DIRECT VS. INDIRECT COMPETITION

In virtually all studies done on female preferences in computer games, puzzle games, such as *Tetris,* and racing games, like *Pac-Man,* are at the top of the list. These are examples of indirect competition games. Players do not act directly on their opponent in order to influence the outcome of the game. Gymnastics is also a good example of indirect competition. The competitors are not allowed to do anything that directly prevents other competitors from performing their exercises. Instead, each competitor competes against themselves to earn a score. This score is then compared with the other competitors' scores, and the highest ranking wins. Similarly, *Pac-Man* is indirect competition. The players compete to see who can travel farthest within the maze without being 'killed,' yet they cannot directly act upon the each other to affect the outcome.

3.5   APPLICATION OF CONCEPT

At first thought, the concepts of indirect competition and nontraditional conflict situations may seem difficult to incorporate into game design. The traditional game genres are almost all directly competitive and based on traditional conflict situations. In a flight sim, players shoot at each other. In an FPS, players shoot at the 'bad guys.' In an RTS game, players move troops to take control of territory from another player. Can these genres be adjusted or adapted to allow for indirect competitive play without harming the integrity of the gameplay?

The answer is yes, but it will require designers who are willing to think creatively and outside of traditional boundaries. In most cases, the solution is not to remove the direct competition or the head-to-head conflict resolution method, but to provide alternative solutions on an equal basis. Fortunately, there are some examples that can be used as a springboard.

Probably the easiest genre to include these sorts of elements in would be the action/adventure and role-playing genres. These titles are already story based, which provides opportunities for designers to build in options. *Ultima VII Part Two, The Serpent Isle* was an RPG that was consciously designed to provide alternatives to direct competition. According to Lisa Smith, a designer on *The Serpent Isle,* each conflict point was engineered to give the player at least two options. One option was a directly competitive solution, such as the player simply fought the monsters until they were dead. The other would be an indirect or nonconfrontational solution, such as providing the monsters with food to distract them, allowing the player to pass unharmed. This sort of conscious attempt to design outside of traditional definitions resulted in a computer game with such depth and broad appeal that it sold over 100,000 units and was nominated as 1993's RPG of the year by *Strategy Plus Magazine.*

FPSs and fighting games, though, are more of a challenge when designing for a broad audience. These genres are probably the most directly competitive, head-to-head style of game. The FPS requires the player to shoot at opponents and kill them to win. Fighting games require the player to defeat an opponent in hand-to-hand combat. However, there are ways to adapt both of these genres to allow for indirect competition.

A good example of a game that took the traditional genre, FPS, and expanded on the concept of conflict was the groundbreaking title, *Ultima Underworld, The Stygian Abyss*. Released in 1992, this game contained many of the now familiar FPS traits, such as a first-person viewpoint over a hand wielding a weapon, multiple weapons to choose from, and an ultimate goal of regaining control of an area by eliminating the 'bad guys.' What made *Stygian Abyss* so different was that it also provided a well-crafted story that encouraged the player to attempt methods of conflict resolution other than direct confrontation. In fact, there were points in the game where, if the player killed what at first appeared to be an enemy, it would result in difficulties later on. The game also contained indirect elements, such as actions that had to be completed within a set time limit, or skill that was declared successful depending on how well it was performed. All of these elements were skillfully woven into an FPS-style game that went on to achieve many awards and is still cited as a landmark title today.

Flight sims and RTS games are probably a bit more difficult when it comes to incorporating indirect competition and nontraditional conflict resolution styles into their designs. For either, the most obvious method would be to add a deep story. But if that is not possible within the scope of the project, then simply working to provide alternative, equal options for the player could dramatically expand the audience. It is not necessary to change the entire scope of the title to nonconfrontational missions. Even the addition of a couple of missions that offered alternative solutions would not only add interest for the traditional player, but would perhaps open up the title to the nontraditional market.

In the case of the flight sim, precision flying missions could be added to the standard battle missions. These missions would require a player to perform exact or complicated flying patterns in order to achieve a goal. Probably the most famous example of this type of mission shows up in the popular culture film, *Star Wars*. In the final battle scene, Luke Skywalker must precisely guide his X-wing fighter through the trench of the Death Star. Using only 'the force,' he must avoid enemy fire and precisely fire a single missile at the exact spot required to destroy the Imperial space station.

For the RTS titles, which are traditionally about conflict over territory, designing scenarios that provide a slightly different sort of conflict will require some thought. Perhaps missions could be added in which the player must get to an NPC before the enemy does. The addition of indirectly competitive situations makes the game more interesting to everyone.

With this emphasis on indirect competition and nonconfrontational conflict resolution, designers might be led to believe that violence is unappealing to female players. However, research done in 1995 at Her Interactive revealed that nothing could be farther from the truth.

In that research, junior high school girls were presented with some of the popular fighting games to play. Afterward, they filled out questionnaires. The results overwhelmingly showed that the girls didn't like the fighting games. When asked why, their answers were surprising. Their distaste had nothing to do with violence and gore. It had to do with the fact they lost interest in fighting the same opponents over and over again for no good reason. In short, they found the games boring.

Therefore, if a designer is going to put violence into a game and wants improve its appeal to a broader audience that includes females, then two things should be kept in mind: first, make sure there is a reason for the violence, other than achieving the 'win' outcome. Second, consider occasionally providing an alternative solution to the violence.

From the details covered in this chapter, it is clear that a developer must start with the very heart of a game's design—the conflict scenario upon which the game is based—when deciding what audience is being targeted. While the traditional concept of zero-sum games that are resolved through direct competition is certainly valid, their market has also proved to be limited. By thinking outside the traditional norms and adding or adapting these concepts to include indirect competition, nonconflict-based scenarios, and non-gratuitous violence, the designer can begin to move toward producing titles that will appeal to a broader audience and capture a larger market share.

REFERENCES

[Hanscome95] Hanscome, Barbara, "Beyond Chrome and Sizzle," *Game Developer,* February 1995.

[Lewis98] Lewis, Michael, *Sugar, Spice, and Everything Nice, Computer Games Girls Play,* (1998), available online at *http://www.slate.msn.com/id/2713/.*

[Neilsen90] Nielsen, Joyce McCarl, *Sex and Gender in Society, Perspectives on Startification,* Waveland Press, Inc., Illinois, 1990.

[Sanday81] Sanday, Peggy Reeves, *Female Power and Male Dominance, On the Origins of Sexual Inequality,* Cambridge University Press, New York, 1981.

CHAPTER 4

STIMULATION AND ENTERTAINMENT

OPS COMMANDER:
ALEXANDRA BLUE

MISSION TARGET:
RESCUE TEAM LEADER

In addition to the physical differences between men and women, there are many physiological differences. Male brains average 11%–12% more in weight than female brains [Chudler]. Men have greater burst strength, while women have better endurance [Ebben98]. Another difference, which can be very valuable to game designers, is the difference between male and female stimulation responses. Understanding the different stimulation types and the response each elicits is a valuable tool for building motivation and interest in computer game titles.

4.1   THE MALE STIMULATION RESPONSE

According to most dictionaries, stimulation is the act of exciting to action or growth. A stimulus is something that arouses or incites to activity, or an agent that directly influences the activity of a living organism (e.g., exciting a sensory organ, or evoking muscular contraction or glandular secretion). What causes this arousal is different for each gender. For males, a visual stimulus results in a physiological response. Males get a measurable physiological reaction from visual input. There is an increase in pulse rate, respiration, and perspiration.

It's fairly easy to see how their reaction evolved. In the earliest forms of human society, the males predominantly served as the hunters, and females were the gatherers. Reproductive characteristics also played an important role in the evolution of these roles. As was mentioned in Chapter 3, adult, premenopausal females spent the majority of their time either pregnant or lactating, neither of which are suitable physical conditions for a hunter—it's hard to bring down a wildebeest when you are eight months pregnant!

In this type of society, hunting was certainly the more dangerous occupation. Hunters could be injured or even killed by their prey.

This made the occupation unsuitable for the adult female who would either be carrying a child, nursing a child, or simply have the potential of producing a child. If the female died in the hunt, not only did the tribe lose that female member, it lost the child(ren) who depended upon her, as well as any future children that she might have produced. In contrast, the loss of a male, while certainly detrimental to the tribe, would not have the long-range effect on the tribe's population that the loss of a female member would have. Therefore, the high-risk role of the hunter fell to the male members of the tribe.

Humans quickly moved to the top of the food chain and became an apex predator. As such, we developed a physiology that was suited to that role. We already had eyes that were set in the front of our heads, giving us binocular vision. This visual arrangement is common in predators, as it enables good depth perception and an enhanced ability to judge movement.

While this type of eyesight alone is advantageous, a predator that can react quickly to the sight of the prey would have an even better chance of successfully killing it. For this reason, the visual stimuli produces an adrenaline response in males that increases heart and respiration rates. In other words, the visual stimulus gets the hunter ready for the chase.

These factors made those hunters with the best eyesight and the best response rates more successful; and the more successful hunters passed these traits along to their offspring. The evidence can been seen in the way contemporary males deal with spatial relationships. Research has shown that males excel in targeting a single moving object in an uncluttered environment, such as an antelope running across the plains or a fighter jet in the clear sky [Armstrong-Hall00].

Therefore, the traditional computer game market has a preponderance of titles that emphasize visual stimuli. This has lead to advancements in graphics technologies with profound technological implications. However, it is interesting to note that many times these improvements in graphics abilities have not necessarily been used to improve the actual artistic quality of the images. Instead, their primary focus has been to increase the realism of the action in the game by increasing the visual stimulation through more spraying blood, more flying debris, and more 'moving parts,' in general. This is because this is the type of stimulation that the 'traditional' gamer (males ages 13–25) reacts to most strongly. He wants more visual stimulus [Miller96], and (at the time this book was published) he represents the largest market share of sales revenues.

4.2   THE FEMALE STIMULATION RESPONSE

While females do have the same binocular vision as males, their role as gatherer did not require the development of an adrenal response to visual stimulation. Therefore, females do not have the same physiological response to visual stimuli. It is important to note that this *does not* mean women cannot appreciate good art or visual input. Females can be just as passionately involved in visual stimuli as their male counterparts, and they can appreciate and produce beautiful art just as well as males. They simply do not have the same *physiological* reaction to visual stimulus.

But can a similar physiological response in females be elicited— and if so, what would produce it? And more important, how can game developers harness it? Research shows that to get a similar response from females, there must be also be either emotional stimuli or tactile stimuli [Rescher96] [SfN02].

The traditional way to develop an emotional stimulus is through the use of story. Games that have an emphasis on story, such as the *Gabrial Knight* series by Jane Jenson or the *Myst* series by Rand and

Robyn Miller, have historically had a higher percentage of female players than the market average. The concept of story in games has been discussed and debated for many years, and is a topic unto itself. However, story elements that are relevant here are Non-Player Character (NPC) characterization and the game premise.

The game *ICO* for the PS2 does an excellent job of developing emotional involvement for the player with the NPCs in the game. *ICO's* story is not a complicated one. The player's avatar is a young boy who was born with a mark that requires him to be sacrificed by being locked away in a terrible old castle. When the player escapes the cell, a spirit is encountered who has also been trapped in the castle. The entire gameplay consists of getting the avatar and the spirit out of the castle by traversing mazes, solving puzzles, and occasionally fighting monsters.

But, even with the simple story line, the designers foster an emotional involvement within the game through the use of the ghost NPC. This spirit-like character is that of a young girl. She is weak, unable to defend herself, and unable to find her way out on her own. The player must take the spirit by the hand and try to find the safest way to lead her through the castle. Along the way, monsters attack and try to recapture her. The player character must defend her, and even rescue her if need be, from the monsters.

The story isn't deep or even very original, but the way in which the NPC is presented to the player encourages emotional involvement. The ghost NPC is portrayed as weak, defenseless, and innocent. Left alone, she might wander off and fall prey to dangerous NPCs. She has to be helped up onto ledges and must be encouraged to jump.

This NPC might be seen as too pitiful to rescue, were it not for the fact she does offer the player help. When the player encounters particularly difficult puzzles, she will lead the player to key areas and point out important features that are clues to finding the solutions. She also is the key that must be present to unlock doors within the castle. Therefore, keeping her alive is beneficial to the player for reasons other than just the emotional involvement.

4.3   EMOTIONAL STIMULATION

To develop a game premise that will provide an emotional tie-in for the player, the designer needs to present the player with scenarios that provide 'mutually beneficial solutions' to socially significant situations.

"Mutually beneficial solutions" means that the solution will benefit both the player's character and the NPCs with whom the player's character is interacting. In *ICO*, the player's goal is to safely escape the castle, accompanied by the girl's spirit. In the process, the player finds the spirit can open doors and help solve puzzles. Thus, the solution is mutually beneficial.

Myst has another good example of a mutually beneficial solution. Presented in the first person, players find themselves stranded on a deserted island. While exploring, the players uncover a mystery surrounding the disappearance of the family who lived on the island. What the players discover is that to get off the island, they are going to have to solve the mystery. Therefore, what the player does benefits both the player and the people who had lived on the island.

Providing mutually beneficial solutions to 'socially significant' situations does not necessarily mean solving game-world hunger or bringing peace. It simply means solving a problem that is significant to a group of people. In the case of *ICO*, the player must escape, vanquish the evil queen, and prevent the sacrifice of more children. Obviously, this is significant to the people living in the villages, not to mention to the children themselves.

But it doesn't have to be a problem that big. In *Myst,* the player must solve a mystery that would lay to rest a family tormented by a murder. The family isn't even alive; rather, they are represented through recordings and images. Still, solving the murder brings closure to that particular social unit.

Therefore, to build emotional stimulation in the players, the designers must provide a problem that is of concern to a social group of people, and the solution to the problem must be beneficial to both the player and the characters with which they are interacting. While building a game that provides the proper elements for emotional stimuli in the players certainly isn't easy, the process of adding tactile stimulus is even trickier.

4.4   TACTILE STIMULATION

There is one industry that has been able to tap into the stimuli response with great success. The video arcade industry has undergone an amazing change since its beginnings in the early 1970s. The first arcades were dimly lit places with dark painted walls designed to reduce any interference of light on the video game screens. They were always crowded, because machines were placed close together to maximize floor space and increase the per-square-foot revenues.

Arcade parlors looked like this until the early 1990s. They catered heavily to their predominantly male clientele, and females customers were seldom seen in them. During this time, a female producer at a coin-op arcade company started taking lunch breaks at the local arcades to watch the players' reactions to the company's games. After several visits, the lack of female players became obvious. So the producer set out to observe those females who did frequent the arcades and to record their actions and behaviors. Unfortunately, she quickly discovered that the girls simply weren't playing many of the games at all. They were mostly there to watch as the boys played at the machines.

The usual scenario was that a couple would enter the arcade, with the boy leading and the girl walking beside or behind him. The boy would locate the game he wanted to play and head for it. Once there, he would put his tokens in and begin to play, sometimes keeping up a running monologue for the girl. She would stand behind him and watch as he played. Sometimes, she would wander a bit to watch others play, but she would always return to watch her boyfriend play. If he moved to another machine, she would dutifully follow.

However, in the past five years, a change has occurred. Arcade game designers began to implement much of the "force feedback technology" that was becoming available in the game industry.* They developed games that a player could ride in, sit on, paddle, or steer. They designed games that vibrated when the player was 'hit,' or which bounced the player when they hit a bump. They developed motorcycles that could be ridden and steered by leaning the bike one way or the other, and boats that moved by using an actual paddle. They developed snowboards players could stand on and horses that players could ride—and the arcade owners found their profits increasing beyond what a new game usually brought in. One of the big reasons was because women were beginning to play these games. No longer content to simply sit by and play cheerleader, women began to put their money into the slots and play the games.

---

* Force feedback is technology that allows games to provide tactile feedback through an input device such as a joystick or mouse.

The arcades of today are a far cry from the dark places of yester-year. They are not only well lit and decorated with bright colors, but the majority of their floor space now hosts games that provide some sort of tactile input.

Because it is cost prohibitive to provide, for example, a full-size motorcycle for every game, the amount of force feedback systems that can be used in the computer game industry is limited. However, the console industry has taken some advantage of this approach to stimuli with the 'vibrating' game controller. There are other methods of providing similar tactile stimulation, beyond simple vibration, that would not be beyond the scope of current technology and, if employed, could increase the attraction for female players. Perhaps the game control unit could become warm or cool to the touch in response to specific scenarios, or it could bounce or wobble in different ways.

In the world of PC game development, force feedback technology had been primarily reserved for games that use joysticks. However, there are a number of force feedback mice on the market today, and some recent bestselling games have used this technology with great success. *Black and White*, the groundbreaking title by Peter Molyneux, makes great use of this technology, varying the amount and intensity of the mouse vibration in accordance with what is occurring on the screen. However, these tactile technologies are not widely publicized or reviewed, so the general public is not aware that they are available.

Force feedback is now standard fare in just about all console game controller pads. The technology also exists for the PC mouse, so it is important for designers to know about this option and design their games accordingly. If the PC game industry's use of this technology continues to expand, soon force feedback mice will also be considered a standard feature.

One other area of entertainment that can make use of tactile stimuli is the wireless entertainment industry, and the technology is already available. Most cell phones have a 'vibration' feature that could easily be incorporated into wireless games to add another dimension to gameplay.

So, when you consider that emotional or tactile input generates the same response in females as visual stimuli does in males, it is easy to understand why females would watch *Titanic* numerous times over, or why some women carry their favorite romance book along wherever they go. It is for the same reason that a male will play an FPS for hours on end: the activity is generating a physiological response—increased heart rate, respiration rate, and perspiration rate. The difference between males and females lies only in the type of stimuli that triggers the response. By harnessing this stimuli response in both genders, it is possible to capture both markets.

4.5   APPLICATION OF CONCEPTS

Games are all about stimuli. However, if designers pay close attention to the types of stimuli they are putting into their games and how those stimuli are being expressed, they can take major steps toward opening the markets for their titles.

Tactile stimulus is a technical issue that requires designers to work with their programmers to ensure that this effect is included in the game code. The game events that trigger the response must then be identified.

Emotional stimulus, however, is something that the designers can control. They need to keep the concept of mutually beneficial solutions to socially significant situations in mind, implying that they might have to build a complex story into their games. While this is fairly easy for genres that are already story based, such as RPGs and action/adventure titles, there are some genres that do not inherently have story elements, such as FPSs, flight sims, RTSs, and sports titles. However, with a little planning and attention to the title's 'backstory,' it is possible to add an emotional element without having to drastically change the genre or hurt the integrity of the title.

THE BACKSTORY

Backstory refers to the background behind a creative work. While fiction authors would never consider starting on a new work without doing the backstory first, it is often an element that is overlooked completely in game development, particularly in genres that do not traditionally have strong story elements. But all games have motivation; otherwise, no one would play them. Therefore, developing a detailed backstory can help a designer find and develop the emotional tie for their title.

This is where the concept of a mutually beneficial solution to a socially significant problem comes into play. It is the starting point for developing a title's backstory, particularly for nonstory-based genres, such as flight sims and RTSs.

First, for a solution to be mutually beneficial, there must be other characters involved. This does not mean actual NPCs must be present. Characters can be implied and still be effective. For instance, if the title is a flight sim, then the designer should specify who or what it is that the pilot must save, or what the benefit of the mission is. This does not mean the player has to directly interact with these people or objects. For example, if the game is about fighting aliens that are trying to take over the player's home world, the designer could provide references to the 'folks back home.' This can be as subtle as a small photo of a Little League baseball team tucked onto the corner of the pilot's control screen. Or it could be a comment to the wing-man: "Wow, that was really dangerous!" to which the wingman replies, "I don't care. My sister was on Regulith." The player does not know the character's sister, and may not know what or where Regulith is, but the wingman's reply indicates a socially significant problem. These clues provide the players with reference points that indicate there is much at stake, and there are real people who will benefit from their victory.

Building emotional ties in an RTS title might be a bit more tricky. It is difficult to provide a compelling reason why imperialistic behavior is beneficial for any goal other than for monetary gain. However, with a bit of planning and careful backstory building, it can be done. Perhaps the player's lands that have been captured are actually an ancestral homeland being reclaimed; or allusions to a home world can be presented—a world that was destroyed, and now this new world must be conquered to provide a home for the player's people. While either of these scenarios would provide the emotional tie-in that will help boost the title's market appeal, it is important to reinforce the backstory throughout the gameplay. Simply putting it in the introduction or the manual isn't enough. NPCs should comment on the backstory throughout the game. Recognizable landmarks and items that remind the player of the cause also help to build the their motivation.

FPSs and the fighter games might be even more difficult for emotional tie-in design than the RTSs. These titles traditionally rely on their visual stimulus features to capture their audience, and any emotional tie-ins that are provided are more 'shock' based. However, they too can benefit from a little bit of pre-planning and backstory.

First person shooters traditionally emphasize 'macho' characters. *Duke Nukem 3D* is probably the most classic example of a game with the cliché FPS avatar. It would be silly to have Duke get sentimental about his kid in Little League back home, and it would certainly be a drastic change to the title. However, in *Duke Nukem: Land of the Babes*, the Duke is out to save the world and rescue all the women who have been kidnapped from his planet by aliens. To develop more emotional tie-in, a bit of information about the women could be provided, such as who they are and why they should be rescued. By providing the player with this information, the women become more human and more real to the player, and an emotional tie-in is provided without compromising the title.

Fighting games have attempted to build emotional tie-ins by starting with meta-stories. Unfortunately, the meta-story is often not apparent to the player. The characters in fighting games are often designed specifically to showcase their particular fighting style, and their backstory is of lesser priority. This often results in a story that is unwieldy, awkward, and becomes a collection of dissimilar parts that have been cobbled together. Rather than being an asset to the game and providing a solid emotional tie-in, these stories can actually leave a player feeling disjointed and confused.

Again, if a cohesive backstory for the title is developed before the game goes into production, this situation could be alleviated. The designer should first develop the world his/her characters will be coming from. Specifying the planet, continent, terrain, and environment will all aid in developing the type of characters that will come from each area. The characters, while unique, should all seem to come from the same realm of reality. Once the designer has developed who the characters are and where they come from, it is important to develop plausible reasons for their involvement—what they are doing and why. Perhaps they are fighting to avenge a relative's death, or perhaps they are fighting to repay a debt of honor. All of these things would provide the mutually beneficial solution required to begin building emotional tie-ins for the player.

If designers spend time on developing a consistent backstory for their titles, it is likely that a socially significant situation will emerge from that design. If the flight sim pilot is fighting to defend his home world, then obviously he and his people will benefit; thus, the problem is socially significant. However, this is a bit harder to realize in a fight title. If the character is fighting to repay a debt of honor, this situation is significant only to him and the person to whom the debt is owed. While this is technically socially significant, it is not as powerful a motivation as if he were fighting to repay a debt of honor for his village. The slightly larger social group involved in the situation provides a much stronger tie-in.

Probably the most interesting part of developing backstory for a title is the knowledge that most of it will never be known by the player. While this may seem, at first, to be a waste of time, the effort *will* pay off. If the designers know a lot of detail about the world and the characters they are developing, their clues to this game world will seep into the design and infuse the game with a sense of cohesiveness and continuity that will help the players build emotional ties to the games. When done properly, the addition of a backstory will open up the title to new audiences who seek this sort of stimulation, while maintaining the game's integrity for those fans who already find it enjoyable.

When designers begin to consciously consider the differences between male and female stimulus response and apply that information to the games they are designing, they will find they are not only broadening the potential audience for the title, but their titles will be richer, deeper, and more appealing for their target audience, as well. Whether it is the addition of backstory to a flight sim or the technical addition of force feedback to an RPG, addressing alternative stimuli in titles builds player motivation and helps sustain their interest.

REFERENCES

[Armstrong-Hall00] Armstrong-Hall, J. Gail, Ph.D., *Help Your Child Be Spatially Complete, Understanding and Practicing the Male Spatial Skills*, Cader Publishing, Michigan, 2000.

[Chudler] Chudler, Eric, Ph.D., "She Brains – He Brains," in Neuroscience for Kids, available online at *http://www.faculty. washington.edu/chudler/heshe.html.*

[Ebben98] Ebben, William P., MS, MSSW, CSCS, and Randall L. Jensen, Ph.D., "Strength Training for Women: Debunking Myths That Block Opportunity," *The Physician and Sports Medicine* (May 98), Vol. 26, no. 5.

[Miller96] Miller, Leslie, Melissa Chika, and Laura Groppe, "Girls' Preferences in Software Design: Insights from a Focus Group," *Interpersonal Computing and Technology; An Electronic Journal for the 21st Century* (1996), Vol. 4, no. 2.

[Rescher96] Rescher, Brigitte and Peter Rappelsberger, "EEG Changes in Amplitude and Coherence During a Tactile Task in Females and Males," *Journal of Psychophysiology, an International Journal*, Vol. 10, no. 2, Hoegrefe & Huber, Cambridge, MA, 1996.

[SfN02] Society for Neurosciences, "SCIENTISTS UNRAVEL BRAIN CIRCUITS INVOLVED IN JOY AND SADNESS," *http://web.sfn.org/content/AboutSfN1/NewsReleases/am2002_ emotion.html.*

CHAPTER 5

LEARNING AND COMMUNICATIONS STYLES IN COMPUTER GAME DEVELOPMENT

It might not seem very important to consider how players learn when designing a game, but actually it is key to the game's success. When the player first approaches the game, they must 'learn' to play it. This goes deeper than just understanding the rules of the game. It includes learning how to use the interface, how to interact with the game, and how the concept behind the game works.

While everyone has a distinct and specific learning style, general style differences have been noted that distinguish men and women. These learning style differences, when applied to computer game design, can help make a title more appealing to a broader market.

5.1   SPATIAL RELATIONS

From a very early age, differences can be seen in how male and females learn about their environments. Have you ever seen a young boy pick up a rock and throw it at a passing car? While he is usually corrected for this behavior, it is important to know that the boy is developing his spatial learning abilities. Males excel at targeting moving objects in an uncluttered field [Armstrong-Hall00]. Whether they are shooting an arrow at a running wildebeest or scoring a hit on an opposing plane in a flight sim, these are activities that males are comfortable with, and they excel and advance naturally in them.

This spatial learning also extends to navigation. Studies have shown that males tend to use their sense of direction and distance to track an object. And when navigating, they relate to their present position and intended destination by using map-like relations. They navigate better when given directions in precise terms, such as "go one mile west, then turn east and go two and one-half blocks" [Sjolinder].

On the other hand, females excel at targeting stationary objects in a cluttered field. In elementary school, many early lessons involve exercises such as 'locate all the number fives in this picture.' Girls typically do better at these sorts of exercises than males do [Armstrong-Hall00].

Likewise, females use different methods to navigate through an area. Whereas males favor directions, females tend to use landmarks and visual clues. For example, when giving directions to a gas station, a female will use landmarks and descriptions: "Go down to the elementary school and turn right. Then take the first left past the green mailbox" [Sjolinder].

There are many ways these differences can be exploited in computer game development. By offering the player a varied landscape with strategically placed, distinct, and unique details, the female player will feel more comfortable navigating through the territory. For the male player, these landmarks serve as backup navigational items and provide a variety of interesting visual stimuli.

Designers can take advantage of the gender difference in spatial learning by developing missions or quests that involve stationary targeting. Often, this type of game is derogatorily referred to as a "hunt the hot spot" game (the basic idea of which is to move your mouse around the screen until you find the items you can interact with and then click on them). One of the most successful games of all times involves this sort of targeting. *Myst* required players to locate and interact with areas on the screen. Often, the order in which these areas are clicked on, or actions the players took immediately prior to clicking on them, results in a continuation of the plot line through clues or video clips. By using the female's preference for targeting stationary objects in a cluttered field, the designers were able to push their market far beyond the traditional game customer.

This strategy can be applied to other genres, as well. For example, in an FPS, the designer could add levels where the player must shoot the correct target on a wall. In a flight sim, perhaps the player would be asked to bomb one specific building in a field of many similar buildings. This type of design not only appeals to females, but it makes missions more challenging for males by offering them a task that requires using a different type of spatial relationship to successfully complete.

5.2   RISK TAKING

In an arcade parlor, it's not unusual to see a young boy race up to a machine, throw his token in, and begin pounding on the keys while hollering over his shoulder at his friends: "How do I play this?" This is a perfect example of another facet of male learning. Males are more willing to take a risk to learn the provided challenge. They prefer to learn by doing. On the other hand, females are less willing to take risks when learning; they want to know how something works before they attempt it [Gottfried86].

In the arcade where boys are playing, it would not be unusual to see one or more girls hanging back, watching the attract loop on another machine. They are trying to figure out how the game is played before they drop their tokens in. Because the attract loops are not usually designed as learning features, a girl might not be able to figure out how the game is played, and she will often simply walk away.

This difference in learning is a bit harder to deal with when designing games. In fighting games, hidden moves are designed to be 'found' by the players once they are playing the game. For the male players, this is exactly the sort of learning they prefer. Experimenting to find the moves comes naturally; it is a challenge they enjoy.

However, for the female who wants to know how it works before she starts, this is potentially a barrier. Because finding them requires experimentation and 'learning by doing,' females are not as likely to locate them. Thus, the female will be at a disadvantage when playing and may not experience the full play value of the title, and it is unlikely she will return to play the game again.

As was mentioned in Chapter 1, this topic was being discussed on the Women in Game Development mailing list in the summer of 2002. One of the women had purchased a fighting game, and played it until she felt she was good enough to play her boyfriend. When she did, however, he won the game easily, using moves she had never seen before. He had learned the hidden moves by 'just pushing the buttons a lot.' The woman, feeling disheartened and stupid, never played the game again. If this attitude occurs among women who are professional computer game designers, how much stronger must this attitude be among women in the general population?

This does not mean that a game can't have surprises in it. Broad-market games can certainly have surprises, but they should be in the content and context of the game. These surprises should not involve the technology or mechanics of making the game work. For example, it is fine to have a secret door, behind which is a Magic McGuffan or magical device that helps the player solve the game. These surprises can provide interest, a challenge, and a sense of reward for the player. However, it is not a good idea to have a secret door that the player can only find by hitting certain keys on the keyboard in the correct order. Keep surprises in the game, not in the hardware.

To design games that appeal to both genders, designing an extremely intuitive interface is a top priority, and will lessen the amount of experimentation that is needed to play the game. This does not mean the game has to be 'dumbed down' or made 'easier.' On the contrary, development of computer interfaces has become a discipline of its own. Classes in designing intuitive interfaces are now offered in the majority of respected computer science programs. By having a smooth interface, the designer allows the player to get past the technology and right to the content of the title.

5.3   ELECTRONIC COMMUNICATION STYLES

How a person communicates electronically can have a major effect on how they learn about a particular piece of software. Conversely, how the designer of the title communicates electronically to players can have an effect on how well the players learn to interact with the title.

The University of Phoenix online division did a study among students taking courses to find out how males and females learned when online. The fact that students had equal access to materials and instructors led the researches to believe they would see an evening out of gender differences [Blum99]. They found that, instead of a leveling of the results, the gender lines were even more distinctly drawn. These differences were manifested through the students' postings on a class bulletin board. While there were differences noted in many areas, such as the sender's position and writing ability, the most interesting differences occurred in tone, domination, and frequency.

The tone of the female communication was inevitably one of empathy and of wanting to 'make a connection' with their fellow students and instructors. To this effect, they produced messages that were more elegant in their use of language. They used 'tag' words and phrases, such as 'isn't it'—"It's cold today, isn't it?"—to make connections with their fellow students or instructors. Females also were 87% more likely to use emoticons, such as <G> or ☺, to reinforce the nonoffensive tone of their correspondence [Blum99].

Males, on the other hand, used a rougher tone in their communications. Their messages contained harsher language and often conveyed a sense of absolute certainty. Their messages were far more likely to contain a 'put down' of the person to whom they were communicating [Blum99]. The University of Phoenix researchers found that males tended to use these communication techniques to exert dominance over the learning situation, sometimes for a period of several days. Only after a female had interjected a message into the males' conversation did more females become involved in the discussion. However, the study showed that time and again, female input to a discussion was stopped short by a male message. These messages were usually sexual or harsh in nature, typically containing a lengthy joke of a sexual nature that contained a female put-down. This not only stopped all females from being involved in the conversation, it stopped all the females from posting on any discussion for several days. In this way, males in the group 'silenced' the females and took control of the learning situation [Blum99].

An interesting side note, when some females attempted to communicate more like the males, it did not result in greater acceptance. These females ended up being ostracized by both the male and the female participants, and were thus shut out completely [Blum99].

To prevent this type of barrier from keeping females away from computer games, designers need to be aware of the power that 'put-downs' and sexual jokes have in pushing away female players. While male players might enjoy the humor (or at the very least ignore it), female players might walk away permanently, without saying a word, and without buying the title.

Designers also need to be aware of the tone of their communication with the player. To keep the female player involved, communication needs to contain some elements of empathy. It should give her the feeling that someone is communicating 'with' her, not 'at' her.

This can be done through game dialog, tutorial screens, and even the manual for the game itself. Keeping these points in mind will help the female player feel comfortable and keep her coming back to the game again and again.

5.4 APPLICATION OF CONCEPTS

All of these concepts—learning style differences and communication issues—can be applied across the board to virtually all genres of computer games. Theories of learning styles, risk taking, spatial relations, and communication all supercede the boundaries of genre. Understanding these differences and being aware of them while designing will help to broaden market access to the title without compromising the integrity of either the title or the genre.

INCORPORATING SPATIAL RELATION

The most obvious application of spatial relation would be in flight simulators. As mentioned earlier, males excel in targeting moving objects in uncluttered fields, while women excel in targeting non-moving objects in cluttered fields. Flight sims traditionally emphasize the male spatial relation style by mostly consisting of dog fights. Adding missions that emphasize another spatial relation skill, such as precision bombing runs, not only addresses a different market, but also provides a stepped-up challenge for those players by presenting a situation for which the solution requires them to exercise a skill that does not favor one of their strengths.

Applying this sort of gameplay to flight sims is fairly straightforward, while applying it to other genres requires a bit more thought on the designer's part. For the FPS, the situation can be resolved in a manner similar to the flight sim. The player can be given an opportunity to perform precision shooting or be required to locate particular objects in the game in order to receive bonuses. Perhaps a new weapon can be constructed from parts found in crates in a storeroom; however, the parts can only be safely retrieved by shooting the locks off the crates. If the crates themselves are shot, they explode, resulting in a setback in the game's progress. Like the precision bombing runs for flight sims, this would address a different spatial learning style, while providing a challenge that does not cater to the strengths of the other learning styles.

USING HOT SPOTS

The concept of 'hunt the hot spot' has been a staple of the RPG genre for quite a while. In fact, in the early 1980s, the introduction of hot spots was considered a significant advancement in computer game design. However, this technique has fallen by the wayside, and it is now considered a noncreative way to handle design. The challenge for the designers is to develop creative new ways to use the hot-spot concept. This will not only provide a fresh look for a traditional technology, but also provide a play model favoring the strengths of the female players.

In RPGs, hot spots have traditionally been used only on items that are plot specific, resulting in unimaginative play. Essentially, all the player has to do is move the cursor over the screen until it changes, and then click that spot. This is not necessarily a failing of the hot spot-oriented game. Rather, it is a lack of creativity on the part of the designers. Hot spots don't have to be strictly plot related. One of the fascinating things about the single-player *Ultima* series was that the designers set out to make everything in the world actually usable, even if it had nothing to do with the major story arc, such as the player's ability to bake bread. When a player moved the mouse over the oven, it showed up as a hot spot. However, it didn't automatically make bread when clicked on. The players had to figure out how to make the bread. Thus, there was a hot spot, but the player wasn't certain what it did or why it was hot, or if it was even pertinent to the story line. This was a brilliant piece of design based on standard hot-spot technology. Creatively implemented hot spots not only appeal to the female spatial learning method, but can be very beneficial to the scope and general gameplay of the title.

IMPLEMENTING RISK TAKING

The concept of risk taking in learning styles should be addressed not so much in gameplay, but in the mechanics of how the player interacts with the title. It begins with the game interface. Take, for example, the veteran female game player who anxiously awaited the release of the FPS title, *Thief.* The first day it appeared on the store shelves, she rushed out and bought a copy. When she got it home and opened it, she found a 'cheat sheet' of all the keyboard commands that were required to make the game operate—some intuitive, some not. The sheet was very long. After reading the instruction manual, she found she didn't understand the reference card any better. She put the game on her bookshelf without installing it. She thought, perhaps after she read the manual again, she would understand it better. But she did not, and the game was never played. This game had an interface that was so complicated and nonintuitive that it required an extensive reference sheet, which prevented this female game player from even installing the game. Granted, the publisher already had her money; however, it certainly kept her from purchasing the sequels.

This should in no way be construed to mean that designers need to make less complicated or 'dumber' games solely for the sake of the female audience. Females are quite capable of learning and enjoying complicated games. What it does mean is that designers need to consider ways to present the information in an intuitive manner. Due to the incredible popularity of the Internet, Web-based companies have done much research in this area, particularly in regard to the 'average' computer user. It would benefit a game company to consider retaining the services of a professional interface designer with experience in broad market applications to help ensure the accessibility of their game interface.

COMMUNICATING WITH THE PLAYER

Not only the interface needs to be intuitive, but the documentation needs to be intuitive, as well—even personal. Females are more comfortable when communicating in a polite, empathic way, so the manual needs to be presented in a more casual, 'friendly' tone.

In 1995, Her Interactive was conducting a series of focus groups on their title, *McKenzie and Co.* They were testing the installation of the game to ensure the younger audience could install the game easily. The installation information was featured on an Install Guide card, separate from the main game manual. Initially, the manuals were done in the traditional style and presented the information in a straightforward manner. The girls passed it over and went right to the installation guide. In the second round of testing, the new manual had been completed and was included with the boxed game. Testers noticed immediately that the girls in the second focus group spent much more time reading the manual, even though the installation information wasn't in it. They actually referred back to it during the gameplay, something the testers hadn't seen the first time. So, what had made the difference? The manual had been redesigned to look like a high-school yearbook, and the information was presented in a 'fun' and casual style, as if being narrated by the characters of the game. Communication within the manual addressed the player directly and used language one might expect to hear from high-school freshmen. Overall, the second group was more successful using the game, partly because they paid more attention to the manual.

DON'T HIDE THE GAME WITHIN THE TECHNOLOGY

The other potential barrier to a broad market is the practice of hiding the game within the technology. Typically this occurs in fighting games where secret moves are hidden within the game controls. Not only are these moves 'secret,' but these secrets are closely kept by the players themselves. Players delight in springing these moves upon opponents who may not have found them yet. This use of the risk-taking learning style of male players has essentially become a hallmark of the fighting game. However, it is not attractive to the female gamer and, as previously discussed, can actually be a barrier to the game. Is it possible to overcome this and still maintain the integrity of the genre? Yes it is.

There is an unwritten design rule that says every puzzle within a computer game should also have its solution found within the game. This goes for all puzzles, even the ones that seem obvious to the designers, and for two reasons. First, it prevents the players from becoming too frustrated. Second, it prevents the player from leaving the game to find the answer. While this has primarily been applied to RPGs, fighting games can benefit from this rule, as well.

By providing hints and clues to all the secret moves within the game, the designers can begin to address the broader audience's concerns—that of not being able to find the moves. There might be areas the character can punch or kick that will reveal hints, or the player may receive 'tokens' upon winning a game that will open secret vaults of knowledge and provide secret move information. This type of design expansion would certainly help the genre expand its market.

When designers become aware of how females prefer to communicate electronically, it becomes both a challenge and a warning. Attempting to build emotional ties into dialog or instructions is a challenge and must be handled carefully, lest it sound fearful or timid. It is important to understand that there is a difference between language that is friendly and seeks emotional consensus, and language that is overly hesitant. Conversely, language that uses tag lines in a leading way could be seen as patronizing. Thus, it is important to pay careful attention to the language of the game, be it in character dialog or in game option screens. It may not be possible to add tag statements in all places in a game. For instance, a designer certainly wouldn't want to have a 'save game' screen that said, "Save here, OK?" However, it may be possible to adjust the tone of the screen, from "Save Game Screen" to "You may save your game here." This does not change the message, nor does it alter the tone of the game. It simply adds a bit of personalization to the information, thus making it a bit more acceptable to a broader market.

More important to the issue of female communication is that harsh language that puts down females, particularly in the form of sexual jokes, will cause females to cease interacting with the product. This is a key piece of information for developers. Duke saying "Shake it, baby" in *Duke Nukem 3D* is funny to the majority of male players, however it is exactly the type of thing that drives female players away in droves. Designers need to balance their catering to a market that enjoys coarse sexual humor based on female put-downs against the (female) money that the title is driving away. Does this mean that games have to be squeaky clean? Certainly not. It is possible to have sexual humor that does not put down females. For instance, "A woman sees her friend is crying, 'Why are you so sad?' she asks. 'Because I am still a virgin!' the friend says. 'How can that be? Your husband is young, handsome, and strong!' she says. 'But he's a game programmer,' says her friend. 'Every night he sits by the bed and tells me how great it's going to be!' " This joke is humorous not because of gender bias, but because it pokes fun at game programmers. It would be funny even if the genders were reversed.

If designers feel that sexual humor is necessary to their title, then they need to make sure the humor is indeed funny to *all* players, not just the males.

REFERENCES

[Armstrong-Hall00] Armstrong-Hall, J. Gail, Ph.D., *Help Your Child Be Spatially Complete, Booklet I, Understanding and Practicing the Female Spatial Skills,* Cader Publishing, Ltd., Michigan, 2000.

[Armstrong-Hall00] Armstrong-Hall, J. Gail, Ph.D., *Help Your Child be Spatially Complete, Booklet II Understanding and Practicing the Male Spatial Skills,* Cader Publishing, Ltd., Michigan, 2000.

[Blum99] Blum, Kimberly Dawn, "Gender Differences in Asynchronous Learning in Higher Education: Learning Styles, Participation Barriers and Communication Patterns," *JALN,* Vol. 3, No. 1, 1999.

[Gottfried86] Gottfried, Allen W. and Catherine Caldwell Brown, *Play Interactions, The Contribution of Play Materials and Parental Involvement to Children's Development,* Lexington Books, Missouri, 1986.

[Sjolinder] Sjolinder, Marie, SICS, *Individual Differences in Spatial Cognition and Hypermedia Navigation,* available online at *http://www.sics.se/humle/projects/persona/web/littsurvey/ch5.pdf.*

CHAPTER 6

REWARD AND GAMEPLAY

In many traditional computer games, the score or level that the player has achieved is prominently displayed on the screen. Players compete to beat the high score or to advance another level. Players are rewarded for advancing in the game by being given additional challenges, or they are motivated to continue playing by offering them the opportunity to beat their most recent score.

6.1   SCORES AND LEVELS

However, these types of incentives are not always appealing to female players. An interesting insight resulted from a survey of junior-high-school girls done for internal use in 1995 by Her Interactive. In this survey, girls were asked how they felt about the violence in games—fighting games, in particular. Eight-six percent of the girls responded that they didn't mind the violence, itself, in the games. What they didn't like was the repetitive nature of the violence. "I beat the guy and ripped his heart out once," one of the girls responded. "Why would I want to do it again?"

A study, *Girls Preferences in Software Design: Insights From a Focus Group*, done at Massachusetts Institute of Technology (MIT) showed more interesting information. This study revealed that while boys are strongly motivated to achieve the highest scores possible, girls place much less importance on it. Not only was the score unimportant to them, but who won and who lost was also not seen as important [Miller96].

So, if the score of the game isn't important, and if who wins and who loses holds little interest, what rewards *do* intrigue females?

6.2   RESPONSE TO ERROR

The beginning of the answer lies in Kafi's study done at MIT, described in Chapter 1, in which children were divided by gender and asked to develop a math game to teach. The children worked within their groups and were given free reign for developing their concepts. As noted in Chapter 1, there were very distinct differences in the completed designs, such as how the games dealt with failure. In the boys' games, failure resulted in the character's 'death.' The player was sent back to the beginning of the game to start over from scratch. In contrast, the girls' games handled failure by temporarily stopping the player's progress in the game. In once case, the character was briefly prohibited from continuing down a the ski slope; in another, a puzzle piece was withheld until the player tried again and succeeded—but none of the games resulted in 'death' or the need to start from the very beginning. In the games developed by the girls, the player was forgiven for their error, while in the boys' games, the player was punished for their error [Miller96].

Brenda Laurel points out in her research that females do not care for the 'step and die' style that many console titles employ. Females want the ability to take a chance without an error being 'terminal' [Dumett98].

6.3 COOPERATIVE PLAY

Study after study has referred to females as preferring cooperative play; but what does this mean, exactly [Children00] [Garvey90]? In cooperative play, players work together to achieve an agreed-upon goal. This type of play inherently means that cooperation, compromise, and negotiation skills are all used to achieve this goal. In Garvey's work, play research shows that among young children, girls were more likely to work together to plan their play and were very attentive to each other's ideas [Garvey90]. Boys, on the other hand, were more likely to switch pretend topics as they played, with each boy attempting to control the group's activities by imposing his own play plan. Boys also engaged in more solitary pretend activities than girls did. It is also interesting to note that the boys were more likely to enact their pretend plans, while girls did more elaborate planning, but did not act on those plans as often.

This suggests that for the females, negotiating the game strategy with others was equal to, if not more important than, actually playing the game itself. In fact, it was *part of* the gameplay; developing a strategy for gameplay that was satisfactory to all members of the group was often a goal unto itself. This tells designers that the female player is very concerned with their fellow players' 'happiness' with the gameplay, even if the fellow player is an opponent.

For example, when employees at American Laser Games (Albuquerque, NM) received a new *Mortal Combat II* arcade game, a company tournament was immediately set up, and before long, a 'champ' was crowned. Shortly thereafter, one of the programmers brought his sister into the office to play. He said she was pretty good, and asked if anyone wanted to play her. The office champ jumped at the opportunity. In five minutes, the girl had thrashed him mercilessly. As she won the last round, he slapped at the machine and turned to stomp off, muttering under his breath. "Wait" she said, her voice full of concern. "Don't go! Let's play again! I'll play a different character this time, okay?" Clearly the 'win' was not as important as making sure her opponent was happy with the game. She was willing to take a handicap (and probably lose) in order to make sure he enjoyed the game. Thus, while males are comfortable competing for a score or a win/lose result, females are comfortable with a satisfying emotional resolution for the game. This is not an easy concept to incorporate into many of the traditional game genres. As previously mentioned, the majority of games are built on 'zero-sum' activities, obstacles or challenges that must be overcome to achieve a goal that is measured as 'win' or 'lose' (see Chapter 3).

This widely accepted definition of what makes a game must be reconsidered when designers target the non-traditional market. The designer must think of other ways to reward a player instead of, or in addition to, the traditional scoreboard or a win/lose outcome. Several games have done this and gone on to terrific success. The *Sim* line of titles is probably one of the most remarkable of these, and for many reasons. One of the reasons is the amazingly flexible reward system. In all of the *Sim* games, the goal is to build a thriving, interdependent system, such as a town, a tower, or an anthill. How the player chooses to construct this system and what is done with the system after it is operating is pretty much up to the player. The player can choose to build the system as fast as possible, or to build the system as stable as possible. The player can also choose to build the system in such a way that it has the greatest chance of surviving whatever disasters the game provides; or the player can build the system to be wealthy and powerful, and then destroy it on command— much like building a sand castle in order to pour water on it and destroy it.

Each of the choices in the *Sim* games provides a different reward for the player. In the case of building a system that survives game-induced calamities, the player's reward is in 'saving' the system. If the player builds a system in order to tear it down, the reward is in the visual destruction of the system and the feeling of power that the player exercises over his or her creation. In the *Sim* series, building the systems faster equates to the traditional reward of a higher score. Therefore, the reward system is flexible and can take into account the entertainment criteria and play style of many different players.

Peter Molyneaux's *Black and White* is another game that takes different reward criteria into consideration. The player takes the role of a deity and is given a world of followers. How the player chooses to treat the inhabitants of the world will result in what type of deity the player becomes—either a caring "white" god or a destructive "black" god. This allows the player much the same flexibility as in the *Sim* games. The player can choose to build the world up and keep it functioning in the best, most productive manner, or the player can build it up just to destroy it.

6.4 APPLICATION OF CONCEPTS

Black and White and the *Sim* line of games were all initially designed to have alternative rewards in them. However, it is possible to introduce alternative rewards into games that are win/lose oriented. Again, games with a story line, such as RPGs and action/adventure titles, are naturals for these rewards, and often contain reward alternatives in the form of 'side' quest/stories. These additional activities often have no bearing on the main story arc, but provide a sense of satisfaction unto themselves. The *Ultima* PC games were full of these types of activities. The designers intentionally designed activities into the various town locations that had no bearing on the main story line, but they were interesting and fulfilling on their own. These activities ranged from weaving cloth to reuniting a child with a lost pet. None of these activities helped the player advance in the game, but they were all rewarding in their diversity and sense of accomplishment for the player.

Other genres, such as FPS and RTS, are a bit more of a challenge, because they are so inherently score driven. Designers would benefit by stepping back for a look at the world they have created. Are there objects or locations in the world that might invite exploration or experimentation? Sometimes even looking at the tools used to build the game world can provide inspiration. During development of an

RTS title, the designers and programmers at Illusion Machines found that they really had fun playing with their terrain generator. They decided to build specific locations into the world where the player could experiment with the terrain generator. These areas were carefully placed in parts of the terrain map where they could not be exploited and would not affect the overall gameplay. When Illusion Machines held their focus group testing for the title, this feature was a big hit. It allowed the players to experiment with other rewards, and yet did not take away from the overall vision for the title.

The response-to-error concepts are a bit easier for the designer to implement. Arcade games, many console titles, and flight/combat sims deal in 'lives'—the number of chances a player has to get the scenario 'right.' The players can continue to play until they make a fatal mistake and are either placed back at the spot where the fatal decision was made or are sent back to the beginning of either the level or of the entire game. In either case, the player is minus a 'life.'

Her Interactive took a different route with *Vampire Diaries*. In this title, the designers flagged each area where a 'fatal' decision could be made. If the players 'died,' they were sent back to where they were just prior to making the fatal error. In this way, the players could try the same situation again, or they could choose another route all together. There was no limit to the number of times a players could do this; nor were they penalized in any way for the fatal error. Essentially, the players were 'forgiven' for the error, rather than punished.

Ironically, the concept of death and punishment, by making the player start over, is actually an antithesis to good game design. Good design keeps the players in the game, and keeps them playing. By making players start over, the designer forces the players out of the game, which raises the strong possibility that they will not re-enter the game.

The concept of character 'death' has been bandied about at gaming conferences for several years now. Should the player be able to 'die' and then come back again, or will that cheapen the concept of death? Without the concept of death, will the player feel that there is enough at stake to make the game interesting? These questions can provide interesting and lively conversations between game designers, even if no consensus is reached. However, when looked at from the prospective of broadening a market and capturing new market share, the designers need to keep two things in mind. The first is females prefer forgiveness for errors rather than punishment. The second is they prefer a temporary block in progress rather than restarting the game from the beginning.

Overall, to design a game that appeals to a broad market base, a designer has to be able to think outside the traditional definitions of games and take alternative reward systems into consideration. For traditional score- or level-based games, this might require stepping back and looking at the game as a whole, or it might require a close examination of the various locations and areas within the game. In short, it requires designers who are flexible in thought and willing to push the definitions of the various genres to find a unique combination of reward systems that will make their title stand out from the crowd. Through this type of creative thinking, designers will be able to attract new players and garner higher revenues.

REFERENCES

[Children00] "Children Now, Girls and Gaming, Console Video Game Content Analysis," Oakland, California, 2000, available online at *http://www.childrennow.org/media/video-games/video-games-girls.pdf.*

[Dumett98], Dumett Susan, *Microsoft Internet Magazine,* 1996.

[Garvey90] Garvey, Catherine, *PLAY,* Harvard University Press, Cambridge, Massachusetts, 1990.

[Miller 96] Miller, Leslie, Melissa Chaika, and Laura Groppe, "Girls' Preferences in Software Design: Insights from a Focus Group," *Interpersonal Computing and Technology, an Electronic Journal for the 21st Century* (April 1996), Vol. 4, no. 2.

CHAPTER 7

AVATAR SELECTION

Certain game genres, by their very nature, require that the player be visually represented on the computer screen. For RPGs, action/adventure, and fighting games, character portraits are a fundamental part of the genre. This player representation is referred to by many names, such as avatar, toon, icon, or character; the most commonly used term is "avatar." The player's character portrait is this 'face' with which the player interacts with the game world. Likewise, it is this face to which the game world responds. So, if the player has chosen a female character, then all characters in the world will refer to the player as "she."

Because it is through the avatar that the player interacts with the game, it is a key part of making the player comfortable with the gameplay. How the avatar is presented, the roles the avatar is given to play, and how the designer communicates the game through the avatar to the player are vitally important to ensuring the player's comfort level and enjoyment of the game.

7.1   THE EVOLUTION OF AVATARS

In early games like *Asteroids* or *Pac-Man,* player representation was, quite simple, by necessity. In *Asteroids,* the character was represented by a spaceship. Pac-Man was a round ball with an eye. However, as technology advanced, player representation became more detailed. This representation can play a major role in determining the player's enjoyment of a game. A well-constructed avatar will encourage the player to identify with the character, and it will increase the player's comfort level within the game. In turn, this emotional tie and comfort level can create an enjoyable gaming experience, building 'stickiness' and replay quality.

When designers begin to construct the avatar choices for a game, a lot of thought and planning go into the character's statistics and how well the character is balanced. This is crucial to gameplay. In comparison, less time is spent on how the character looks, and even less on the possibility of providing a gender choice. The gender of the avatar might not seem important when compared to other elements of game balance, such as graphic and engine considerations; but it can be a very important issue for female players and can have a huge influence on a female player's enjoyment of the title. In short, if there is no ability to choose a female avatar, or if the female selection is limited or poor in quality, the game will be less attractive to the average female. Terrific game balance, great graphics, and a screaming engine don't mean a thing if the player doesn't feel the game is for her.

7.2   THE PYRAMID OF POWER

The gender issue does not make sense to a lot of male developers who often say they have no problem playing a female character. They cannot understand a female player's discomfort with playing a male character. This discomfort stems not from hypersensitivity, but is actually the result of a sociological concept, called the "pyramid of power" [Sutherland96].

The pyramid of power is a phenomenon that occurs in all cultures and societies in response to their multi-layered power structures. Some people hold more power and have a higher social standing than others; and the higher up in the power structure a person is, the fewer peers they have. In other words, in all societies, there are more people with less power and less people with more power. If we graphically stack the levels of society on top of each other, placing those with less power on the bottom and working up to the most powerful group on top, the result would resemble a pyramid— hence, the pyramid of power (see Figure 7.1).

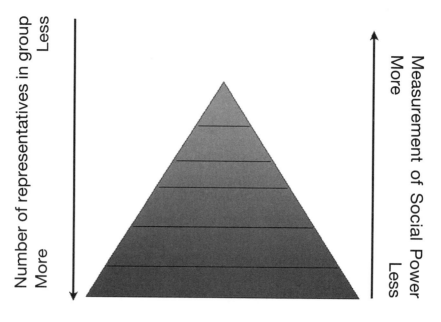

FIGURE 7.1   Pyramid of power.

The pyramid of power can be used to demonstrate power derived from any source or at any level. This can be a ranking of nations based upon their Gross Domestic Product (GDP), or it can be tribe members in Africa based upon the number of cows they own. In its application to computer games and avatar choices, the power stratification based on gender is the key.

The majority of dominant, gender-based societal structures in the world today are patriarchal in nature. In its simplistic form, a patriarchal system is one in which inheritance is based on the male line. When wealth is determined through the male line, then males in that society will have more power than the females. Therefore, in the modern model for most societies, the males are in the upper layers of the pyramid and females are in the lower layers.

While this power structure is true for the majority of cultures, it may not be reflected in some smaller family groups. Female-headed households are becoming more common. However, this does not make members of that household immune from the effects of patriarchy. In their day-to-day lives, they still function in a society that is male dominated, and this is reflected in everything they come in contact with, from schools and businesses to entertainment and politics.

How members of the different layers of the pyramid interact is where this theory becomes important for computer game designers. Within the pyramid, each member of a particular level is comfortable within that level. Comfortable does not necessarily mean happy. It simply means they understand the limits, rules, taboos, and mores society puts upon their particular strata, and they are used to functioning comfortably within those conditions.

The pyramid of power also maintains that people are not only comfortable in their own strata, but they are also comfortable functioning in the levels below their own and do not have a problem with stepping 'down' to fill a role that is beneath them in the pyramid. Again, this doesn't mean they would be happy in that role, they're just comfortable with and understand the rules and regulations put upon them by the that level of the strata.

However, if people are called to function at a level above them in the pyramid, their comfort level decreases. This is because they are not familiar with the societal rules and taboos associated with the positions above their own. The further they move up the pyramid, away from their own position, the more their discomfort increases.

For instance, in a traditional feudal society with peasants, nobility, and royalty, a baron would not have difficulty functioning if he suddenly found himself as the castle's baker. He would probably not be happy with his lot, but he would understand the social rules associated with the tradesman's class and be comfortable functioning within those parameters. However, if the scullery maid suddenly found herself standing in for the king, she would be very uncomfortable; she would not understand the societal rules that define that position.

So, because Western cultures are predominantly patriarchal, and males control the majority of the wealth, they hold the positions of highest power. Therefore, they are above females in the pyramidal structure. It makes sense, then, that it is not uncomfortable for a male player to take on a female avatar, because by doing so, he is simply stepping down a level on the pyramid. However, taking on a male character requires a female player to move up the pyramid and step into a role for which she does not know the rules. This *is* uncomfortable for her.

Sometimes this concept is difficult for male developers to grasp. They have always been at the top of the pyramid structure, a position in which virtually all roles in society fall beneath them. Therefore, they are comfortable with almost any role handed to them. Because they have always been in a position of power, it is difficult for them to relate to a position that is lower on the pyramid. They simply assume everyone else feels as they do.

A very clear example of what happens when people are placed above their level on the pyramid was related by a software engineer from India. She talked to an American woman who had moved to India when her husband had been transferred there. The American woman had some difficulties dealing with the Indian caste system.

She was having some yard work done by a man who was an Untouchable—the lowest level in the Indian caste system (pyramid of power). About halfway through the day, she asked her housekeeper if the man needed to use the restroom. The housekeeper told her that Untouchables were never allowed into the house, let alone allowed to use the restroom indoors. The housekeeper said the yardman would simply relieve himself in the street, as was expected of someone of his caste.

Of course, this went against everything the woman believed in as an American. She insisted the man should be allowed to use the restroom in the house. After several days of coaxing, when she finally got the man into her house and into the restroom, she realized that he wasn't actually using the restroom at all. He was simply standing in the restroom, too uncomfortable to touch a thing.

This is an example of what can happen when someone is asked to function in an area above their power level. The yardman, who was a member of the lowest power strata in the society, was being asked to function in an area that was many levels above him. He didn't know how to act, what was expected of him, or what the consequences of his actions would be; so he simply did as little as possible to prevent any further discomfort.

Of course, in America, the lines of societal structure are much more vague than a caste system, but the power structure is definitely patriarchal, and the interactions between the strata still hold true. A very clear example of this occurred at a prominent game company in the mid-1990s.

A team was working on a FRP computer game. While the stats on all the characters were exactly the same, the game gave the player the opportunity to choose the gender of their avatar. The product was very close to ship date so the entire QA (Quality Assurance) department was testing the product. At that time, the QA department consisted of approximately 20 males and three females. One of the game's designers was working on a particular problem, and went to the QA department to watch the problem area being tested. When she arrived, she was surprised to note that, without exception, the male testers were all using the female avatar to test the game. A closer look revealed that the female testers were, likewise, using the female avatar. The designer made a comment to one of her fellow designers, and the following week they made notes of what genders were being played and by whom. At the end of the week, it became apparent the male testers were simply not using the male avatars, and neither were the female testers. This resulted in a memo to the QA department, asking them to consciously divide their time so that both genders were equally tested.

The designer was intrigued by this and asked the males in QA why they were using the female avatar. Their answer was almost always, "because she is prettier and nicer to look at." When the female members of QA were asked why they were using the female avatar, their answer was usually, "I always play female characters. Playing a male character just doesn't feel right."

Designers certainly don't want to force a player to do something that 'doesn't feel right,' and yet, they may do so unknowingly by providing only male avatars. To make females comfortable with a game and to help make games more appealing to them, it is vitally important to provide avatars that are female. However, it goes further than this. It is also important that the female avatars be equally and fairly represented. This means having all character classes available in both male and female representation, and having the actual representation equitable.

7.3   TOKEN CHARACTER CLASSES

Offering only select character classes in specific genders has been a common practice in computer games for quite a while. The reason for this is often chalked up to limited space. The original *Diablo* offered three character classes: a fighter, a mage, and a rogue. The fighter and mage were male. The rogue was female.

For the male players, this was completely acceptable. They were comfortable with all three characters. However, this was not the case for female players. The only class option open to them was the female rogue. Females that might have been interested in playing the mage or fighter had to overcome a certain amount of discomfort in order to play the game. Unfortunately, people will rarely play games that make them even mildly uncomfortable, so this became a barrier to play for a percentage of the total possible audience.

Not only does this limited offering exclude a percentage of females that may be interested in playing the game, but how those characters are presented may also be distasteful. By limiting the number of female-presenting characters to a fraction of those that are male-presenting, it may also appear that the female character offered is nothing more than a 'token' character, particularly if the character class chosen to be female is stereotypical in its appearance or in its assigned occupation. For instance, if the game is a space combat sim, and the three male-presenting avatars are a marine, a former mercenary, and an aerobatics pilot, and the female-presenting character is a secretary, then the message sent is pretty clear. The female character is not only out of type from the other classes, but it is also stereotypical.

Females faced with this choice of avatar, then, can either be uncomfortable with a male character or uncomfortable with a stereotypically 'weak' female character. This certainly gives the female player the impression that this game was never really intended for her, so she is unlikely to buy or play it. The player might lose out because it may very well be a terrifically designed game, with that one exception; but the company definitely loses out because an entire market share has been pushed away.

7.4   REPRESENTATION OF AVATARS

Fortunately, the storage capacity on computers and consoles has increased dramatically, so the industry is beginning to see more games that offer all of their character classes with both male- or female-presenting options. Unfortunately, the depiction of the female characters can often be less than appealing to a female audience.

The typical female character can be seen in the promo for *Anarchy Online* (Figure 7.2). The female is depicted with unrealistically large breasts, a waspish waist, and a prominent, well-rounded derriere. She is dressed in what is essentially lingerie, which is designed to enhance her exaggerated physical traits. Everything about this hyper-sexualized depiction, from her physical proportions to the way she is dressed, says, "I'm young, fertile, and ready for sex!"

The traits that give off these signals are very specific. For the female form, breasts that are high on the chest, a small waist, and a firm derriere are all indicators of youth. Large breasts and rounded hips are signals of fertility. Likewise, there are physical signals that indicate a female is sexually receptive: blood flows to her face (the blush), and eye and lip size increase, resulting in the reddish, full-lipped pout. Her eyelids will also appear heavier, something often referred to as 'bedroom eyes,' and her nipples will become erect.

In typical female avatar representations, these signals are often ridiculously exaggerated. Often, the player will be offered the choice of a female avatar portrait who's breasts are huge and seem to almost float under the character's chin, has a large, round derriere, and a waist that is smaller than her head. The portrait will have large scarlet lips, sultry eyes, and erect nipples. Sometimes these erect nipples even show through plate armor! Usually, the character will be dressed to emphasize these traits, and even her animations and still frames will be provocative. This type of female avatar depiction is so common that it occurs in almost every genre. At the E3 Expo in

FIGURE 7.2   Ad for *Anarchy Online*. © 2003.
Reprinted with permission from Funcom, Inc.

2002, a golf game was being shown at the Microsoft® booth. One of
the avatars that the player could select was a busty blonde character
dressed in tight jeans and a halter top. Her animation after making a
shot consisted of her leaning forward, one hand on her thigh, the
other on her waist, and provocatively cocking one hip so as to more

prominently display her derriere. Not surprisingly, there wasn't a single male avatar with a similar animation.

But aren't male characters also portrayed unrealistically? Yes they are, but there is a difference. Male avatars are very often presented with exaggerated signals of youth and virility, such as broad shoulders, slim hips, and well-muscled arms. They are not, however, presented as hypersexualized. They do not display anything that indicates sexual receptiveness, such as an erection, red lips, or heavily lidded eyes, and their sexual organs are not enlarged to unrealistic proportions. The clothing they are clad in might often emphasize the large shoulders and slim hips, but is certainly not designed to draw attention to the fact they are sexually receptive.

Male characters are presented as males would like to be in the game—young, strong, and virile. Likewise, the female characters are presented as male players would like them to be—young, fertile, and always ready for sex.

It is extremely unlikely that male players would be comfortable with or enjoy playing a game in which their sexuality and sexual receptiveness was exaggerated to the point of being the main feature of their avatar. And it is certain that design teams would be horrified if someone suggested they present their males characters in the same fashion they present their hypersexualized female characters. It stands to reason then, that women are likewise uncomfortable playing a sexually exaggerated character.

Does this mean that female characters cannot be sexy? Certainly not. But the key difference here is 'sexy,' not 'hypersexualized.' Female avatars can be attractive without being sexual objects. A good example of this would be the character Xena in the television series, *Xena, Warrior Princess*. Xena is a strong and sexy character and who can wield a sword as skillfully as any man. She is attractive without being hypersexualized. Her body proportions are obviously female, but those proportions are not exaggerated. Her clothing, though 'sexy,' emphasizes that she is female but does not dominate the character. Over all, Xena is a character that females can relate to and would want to have represent them in a game.

It is not impossible to make a title that offers equality in avatars. *Ultima VII Part Two, The Serpent Isle* (Origin Systems) was one of the first titles to feature female avatars whose artwork was based upon female athletes. They were strong, lean, and obviously female, but they were not hypersexualized. Their armor and weaponry was not erotic in nature, and in fact, the females did not vary much from the males, except in the obvious externals.

Today, the majority of well-presented female avatars exist in online role-playing games, such as *Ultima Online* or *Asheron's Call*. Their female figures are feminine without being hypersexualized. Their armor is equivalent to the male's in coverage and look, except that it is formed for the female figure. When stripped of all clothing, the female avatar is clad in simple underclothes, not exotic lingerie. It is also interesting to note that currently, the online games have a higher percentage of female players than traditional, single-player titles or console games [Xenakis01].

7.5   APPLICATION OF CONCEPTS

Changing the way avatars are presented is probably one of the least painful ways to open up the market for a title. The avatars have to be developed anyway, so it costs nothing extra to develop art for the female characters that is not hypersexualized. It also does not affect the game context or content in any way. Through this one simple change, it is possible to remove the single largest barrier to attracting a more diverse market share.

Designing a computer game that offers the choice of both male- and female-presenting avatars might be a bit more costly. It does require more art, animation time, and more storage space for the game. There is no easy answer for this question. It becomes a matter of weighing the entire potential of the market versus the initial cost of development. It also involves taking a hard look at the overall design of the game. Simply adding a female avatar for every male avatar may help expand a game's market somewhat, but it is most beneficial when the entire design concept, from the beginning, has been developed to make the most of the audience potential that is out there.

Developers will often cite the increased animation cost as the reason for not offering all characters in both genders. This may be true, and there might not be an easy way around it; however, it could help to make the game appealing to the other 52% of the U.S. population, so the additional cost might well be worth it.

REFERENCES

[Bromhall97] "Language of the Sexes," *Desmond Morris' the Human Sexes*, Clive Bromhall, 1997.

[Sutherland96] Sutherland, Kay, Ph.D. *Sociology of Women*, St. Edward's University, Austin, Texas; February 25, 1995.

[Xenakis01] Xenakis, John, "Online Games for Girls: E-commerce's Next Frontier?" (February 14, 2001), *CFO.com*, retrieved November 10, 2002, available online at *http://www.cfo.com/article/ 1,5309,2110,00.html*.

CHAPTER 8

PUZZLE GAMES

W hen the subject of gender-inclusive games is brought up to developers, one genre that is always mentioned is puzzle games. Usually, the genre is given the nod as being a valid one, and then the conversation drifts to other issues. But the puzzle genre is a strong, quiet market with a broad, stable following. By harnessing this genre, the designer can add yet another dimension to a title that may help expand its overall market appeal.

8.1 DEFINITION OF "PUZZLE"

First, it is important to understand what a puzzle is. According to Alexey Pajitnov, game designer for Microsoft and father of the puzzle giant, *Tetris*, a puzzle is not 'find the key that opens the door.' "A puzzle is an abstract construct," Pajitnov says. "It is small and elegant, and engages the mind" [Pajitnov02].

Scott Kim, a professional puzzle designer, goes on to define puzzles in this way: "A puzzle is a problem that is fun to solve, which means that the goal is to find the right answer. In contrast, the goal of a 'game' is to beat another player. By this definition single player games like solitaire card games are actually randomly generated puzzles" [Kim02]. It is interesting to note that by this definition, any game that does not contain direct competition, such as resource-allocation games, also fall under the definition of 'puzzle.'

The audience for puzzle-style games, both computer and non-computer based, is distinctly female. According to Kim, 70% of crossword puzzle players are female. The reason for this, Kim states, is that puzzles appeal to the diffuse skill of putting things in order, something Kim believes is distinctly female. He also feels that because puzzles lack the violence and action of traditional computer games, they are more appealing to females. According to Pajitnov, his title *Pandora's Box*, which is a beautifully rendered set of puzzles woven into fairy tale and legend, had an approximately 60% female following [Pajitnov02].

8.2 PUZZLES AND THE NONTRADITIONAL GAME AUDIENCE

These observations begin to fall within what we know about female entertainment criteria. Puzzles are indeed non-confrontational. They are an indirect form of competition where the player is competing only against herself. If another player is involved, the competition is indirect and can be summed up as "Can I finish this activity before they do?" or "Can I do this activity better than they do?" Thus, the player is limited by his or her own ability, and the opponents' actions have no direct bearing on the outcome.

However, traditional puzzles are not emotionally engaging. In fact, most would agree they are exactly the opposite. They are coldly logical. They have a 'right' answer. From what we know about female entertainment, females should not be attracted to them, as they have no emotional tie-in. It is here that we must take the idea of what is appealing to females and begin to turn it on its head. The lack of emotional tie-in, combined with indirect competition, may be exactly what does attract females to this type of games.

While emotional ties are what many game designers rely on to bring their players back over and over again, it may often be what keeps the casual female gamer away. Dr. John Hopson, researcher in the Department of Psychological and Brain Sciences at Duke University, believes that female game players identify more closely than males with their character in computer games. Because of this, they are not as willing to take risks in situations where the character might be put in mortal danger [Hopson02]. So, if the female player doesn't feel she has the time or the energy to devote to the character, then she may not be as willing to play the game.

For females, gaming is akin to reading a romance book. If she only has the time or energy to read one page, then she probably won't open the book at all. Without a certain time investment, she cannot immerse herself into the fantasy of the fiction. So when time or energy resources are short, she may not be as interested in the fantastical, emotionally involving world of the computer game and is more likely to turn on a game that will *not* engage her emotionally, and that means an indirectly competitive, non-emotional game, such as solitaire or *Tetris.*

Puzzle genres have the additional benefit of attracting more than just the female audience. They also attract the older, more mature audience of both genders. While puzzle games may have always been a niche genre in the traditional game industry, according to Kim, in the online game world, they are the most popular genre on the casual gaming sites. "The European and Asian markets have always had a larger puzzle audience than the U.S. markets," adds Pajitnov. "They are not as 'game addicted' and want shorter play sessions, so puzzles appeal to them" [Pajitnov02].

Pajitnov believes that while puzzles have been primarily attributed to female games, they are truly gender inclusive. "The reason people say they are for females is because mostly females play them. But that is only because true female titles have not yet been developed. When they are, then puzzles will take their appropriate place, about 15% of the market" [Pajitnov02].

8.3 APPLICATION OF CONCEPTS

Incorporating puzzles into traditional games is not easy. It is one task that Pajitnov has been working on for quite a while. "Story-based games are about suspension of belief. They are entertaining," says Pajitnov [Pajitnov02]. "Puzzles are abstract concepts requiring mental active concentration, and thus there is a tension between the two types of entertainment." He feels that blending the two types of entertainment is a tricky procedure that requires a very smart, creative designer. "Unfortunately, this [combining of puzzle and story] is the only way we will see puzzle games published anymore," said Pajitnov. "Small puzzle games don't sell well anymore. They don't bring in the money, so publishers aren't willing to fund them. So the only way to publish puzzle titles is to find a way to join the two" [Pajitnov02].

Kim says most puzzles can be divided into three types: logic puzzles, word puzzles, and visual puzzles; with computer puzzles becoming common enough to make up a fourth category, which is a combination of visual and logic types. An example of a logic puzzle would be something like the classic puzzle, *Mastermind*. A crossword puzzle is an example of a word puzzle, and a jigsaw puzzle is an example of a visual puzzle. He believes that most players, both male and female, will find themselves attracted to one or more puzzle types. The majority of traditional games today tend to concentrate on just one type of puzzle. However, in order to appeal to the broadest audience, Kim says it is important to incorporate all three types of puzzles into the game design [Kim02].

Pajitnov also feels that the upcoming wireless market may be the next big frontier for the puzzle genre. It is perfect for the small, elegant puzzle concept, because puzzles don't require fancy graphics or sound. He says he is encouraged, as many of the older, standard puzzle games are gaining popularity on that platform. He feels that as the popularity of puzzle games expands into the wireless market, publishers will begin to realize the value of the genre. "Puzzles sell much more moderately than action games. For that reason, they never get a good marketing budget. They are promoted mostly by word of mouth. But, they have a much longer shelf life. An action game gets played once, maybe twice. But a puzzle you can play again and again. It brings in a modest, but much longer term, return" [Pajitnov02].

One method of putting a puzzle into an RPG-style game that has had some success is to have the puzzle represent some mundane action that occurs in the real world. Her Interactive's title *McKenzie & Co* did this, and it was met with moderate success. This title was about getting through a year of high school. The player's character went to school, took tests, went to an after-school job, talked to friends, and faced decisions—such as, should she go to a party or help out her family, as she had promised?

The activities that would not actually be 'fun,' such as going to work or taking a test, were replaced with puzzle activities. For example, the 'test' in science class was actually a visual puzzle where the player was shown an extreme close-up of an insect and, within a certain amount of time, had to match it to the correct complete picture of an insect. The time allowed to make this match was dictated on an 'easy,' 'medium,' or 'hard' setting the player had chosen at the beginning of the game. How well the player did on their 'test' had an actual effect on the game. Low scores in the puzzle game were treated as a low score on the test, and the player was gently scolded by the instructor and assigned additional homework that day.

Additionally, these 'mini-games' were accessible from the start menu of the game, so that a player didn't have to actually play the entire RPG to get to the mini-games. The player could choose to play those games apart from the main game. From the response cards Her Interactive received, it was found that the mini-games were often mentioned as a favorite feature of *McKensie & Co*. The girls seemed to enjoy the games enough in the main game that they would often play them outside the main title.

Puzzles have an appeal that reaches across gender and age lines, and continue to hold the fascination of audiences over a long period of time. For these reasons, puzzles can be one of the strongest tools in a designer's arsenal of ways to expand a title's audience. While developing quality puzzles that stand the test of time isn't an easy task, it's not impossible. And designers need to not overlook the idea of puzzles when they are laying out their game concepts.

REFERENCES

[Hopson02] Hopson, John, Ph.D., Re. Fwd.: "The Psychology of Choice," e-mail to Sheri Graner Ray; November 8, 2002.

[Kim02] Kim, Scott, e-mail interview with Sheri Graner Ray; November 14, 2002.

[Pajitnov02] Pajinov, Alexey, personal interview with Sheri Graner Ray; December 13, 2002.

CHAPTER 9

ONLINE AND WIRELESS GAMES

In 1995, a phenomenon happened in the game development world. *Ultima Online* was launched, and an entirely new industry was born. Online games were a long time dream of Richard Garriot who believed they would revolutionize not only the game industry, but the very way the public played all games. He was right, but *Ultima Online* had repercussions beyond the obvious opening of an entire new field of game development. It also served to broaden the audience base; and for the first time, female gamers were appearing in measurable numbers. Producers and marketers at Origin Systems had long suspected that the *Ultima* titles garnered more female players than other titles in the genre. But with the arrival of the online version, the female players were visible and having an effect on the game world itself.

They didn't flock only to *Ultima Online*. Soon, female players were showing up for the online titles in higher numbers than the traditional game industry had ever seen before—according to industry sources, as high as 15% [Powers03]. What causes this popularity? What do the online titles have that attract the female players, which stand-alone titles don't? Is there something inherent in the real-time medium that is more attractive to the female players?

9.1   THE FLEXIBILITY OF ONLINE GAMES

Although it may not have been a deliberate design decision, online games are very flexible in their design. While they provide some directed play in the form of quests, missions, and story, they are also a type of 'sandbox' in that the developers provide the world, and the players decide for themselves what they are going to do or build in it. Each online game is different, with varying amounts of directed play versus sandbox play. *The Sims Online* is almost entirely a sandbox world where players are left to their own devices to build and play as they wish. *Everquest* and *Anarchy Online* are heavily 'quest' based. In these types of games, players generally advance by completing missions or tasks found within the game.

This balance of sandbox and directed play gives the players much more freedom than in traditional stand-alone titles, and it enables many different types of play styles and patterns to be exercised.

9.2   REWARD SYSTEMS IN ONLINE GAMES

Online games support different play styles through a variety of reward systems. The players who enjoy optimizing their characters to their greatest ability are rewarded by being allowed to do just that. By providing 'guilds' with hierarchical structures, those players that enjoy social play have a system of rewards and accomplishments by which they can measure themselves. Players that simply enjoy the competition of reaching the highest levels the fastest may pursue that path in the games as well. The majority of online games offer some type of Player-versus-Player (PvP) mechanism that allows players to compete directly against other players. Usually, this mechanism will also offer protection for those players that do not choose to play PvP style.

For players who prefer story line involvement, many online games provide 'quests' that include NPCs with a particular story for the players to become involved in or a problem they need the players to solve. Sometimes these stories are so large in scope, they may actually have an effect upon the very world the player is playing in.

9.3   STORY IN ONLINE GAME DESIGN

This type of online social play also provides the emotional stimulation that is so often missing from traditional games. The fact that the player is interacting with real people gives the player an opportunity to build relationships and an identity within the world. For female players this is an enticing facet, and they have taken it to heart.

According to Nicholas Yee, founder of the Daedalus Project, 19% of female players surveyed stated that they felt they had found their best friend in an online game, compared to 7% of the male players; and 33% of female players have in-game marriages, compared to 10% of males players [Yee03].

Female players seem to be more likely to take their online experience outside of the game world. According to Susan Powers, producer at Turbine Interactive, female players are often the ones to build and then serve as Webmasters for the majority of guild Web sites. They are also the ones to write short stories that are set in the fictional world of the game (fan fiction). These stories will usually show up on Web sites dedicated to those particular worlds [Powers02].

Beyond the emotional tie-in, there are other facets of online game worlds that appeal to female players. With the exception of PvP play, the online world is an indirectly competitive one. Players may not, under any circumstance, act directly upon each other to impede that person's advancement. If interference is desired, it must be done through negotiation, manipulation, or compromise. This, of course, fits nicely into a female's preferred method of conflict resolution (see Chapter 3). It is interesting to note that while there are female players who do actively pursue PvP style, the actual percent of the total population is very small, however studies are currently being conducted by the IGDA to determine real percentages.

PvP style and its rewards allow many different types of players to enjoy the online games. "And one thing we have seen over and over again," said Powers, "is that female players do not collapse neatly into only one category. We have female players whose entire play experience is 'power leveling' one character after another, and others who do nothing except bake cookies for social events. Most of them fall somewhere in between, of course. But overall, female players are just as diverse in their play styles as male players" [Powers02].

9.4   IMPROVING THE ONLINE GAME DESIGN

Even with all these advantages of online gaming, a 15% share of female players is still not a large number. What could the online game designers do to improve these numbers?

The Sims, a stand-alone title by Maxis, captured a market that was 50% female [Globe02]. It is expected that *The Sims Online* will capture similar numbers with its release. *The Sims Online* is different from traditional online games in that its gameplay is almost completely sandbox style. There are no missions or quests the player must undertake. There is no story other than what the players build for themselves. This allows relationships to take center stage in the world.

But another factor about *The Sims Online* that needs to be considered is what it is not. It is not science fiction, nor is it fantasy. Much like a soap opera, it is set in contemporary society. This gives female players a chance to test out relationships and relationship-building techniques, as well as interact with friends.

By not being a science fiction or fantasy title, *The Sims Online* breaks the mold for current online games. And in doing so, it has the opportunity to reach a broader audience, simply through its nontraditional setting. According to the National Science Foundation (NSF), only 30% of people surveyed read science fiction books or magazines [NSB02]. However, for the other 70% of the population, *The Sims Online* has the opportunity to break the genre barrier and introduce new players to the game world.

The Sims Online also worked to preserve an interface and tutorial that was consistent with their stand-alone titles. This built in a comfort level for their players that helped them to become immersed in the game quickly and easily.

9.5   INTERFACES AND TUTORIALS IN ONLINE GAMES

For titles that don't have a standard on which to base their interface, the interface and tutorial can become problematic. Because online games are nonlinear and complex in structure, they can be quite complicated to learn. Often, this requires an interface that can handle many different actions and interactions. If designers make this interface too complicated, it can become a barrier to players trying to access the game. Likewise, the ease of the tutorial can make or break a game.

Recently, a game designer decided she wanted to try a popular online game to see how well she would like online games. She bought the original title as well as one or two of the expansion packs. After installation, she attempted to access the game's tutorial. It did not work. She reinstalled the tutorial, hoping that would solve the problem. When that didn't work, either, she went to the online discussion board and asked for help. She was told that the tutorial had never worked, and she was wasting her time to even try. She tried to enter the game and play without the tutorial's help but was quickly discouraged by the level of complexity of the game and the interface. She shut the game off and never tried it again.

In another situation, a writer on the Women in Game Developments list described her experience with a tutorial as frustrating. In this case, after building her character and entering the game, she found herself dropped into a confined 'safe' area, and was then left to her own devices. There was little direction or information other than the implied instructions. She managed to get through it and learn the game, but she said it was daunting and not a pleasant experience at all [WIGD02].

Thus, an intuitive interface and an accessible tutorial is even more important in the online world than it is in single-player games due to the complex nature of the genre itself. By working to develop tutorials that take different learning styles into consideration, and interfaces that are intuitive, the designers can go a long way toward removing barriers to their titles.

9.6 FEMALES AND PLAYER VS. PLAYER GAMES

As previously stated, PvP is not the usual choice of play for female players. However, there are those that do play PvP, and they are quite good at it. A recent thread on an online discussion board between female PvP players revealed, however, that female and male PvP players may not always have the same goals in mind. When the board canvassed for female PvP players, a handful said they had played PvP. When the former female PvP players were asked why they had quit, one of the main reasons cited was an inability of the male PvP players to follow the rules or be good sports [ACDiscussions03].

According to Catherine Garvey in her book, *Play*, girls were shown to spend as much or more time planning and preparing for their play as actually performing the play. On the other hand, boys were more likely to perform the play without involved planning, and each individual member of the group would attempt to impose his own ideas of the rules upon the group [Garvey90]. It would make sense, then, that the female PvP players would be upset by the male PvP players' lack of ability to follow the established rules. Deciding upon the rules up front is important to the female players, and breaking those rules could be seen as an affront to the group. Male players, on the other hand, will each have their own version of the rules and will seek to assert those rules on the others in the game.

Keep in mind that most female players are more comfortable with resolving conflict situations in nonconfrontational ways, and the majority of females prefer an indirect competitive style rather than direct competition. Females like to work out the rules ahead of time and then adhere to them. So, the small number of female PvP players is understandable, and designers should be aware that in promoting a game that has a PvP aspect, it is likely they will not attract a gender-diverse audience.

9.7   WIRELESS ENTERTAINMENT

Along with online gaming, another new form of electronic entertainment is opening the market to players outside of the traditional audience. Wireless entertainment, which is playable on cell phones, has become increasingly popular as the availability of cell phones has increased.

Anne-Marie Huurre, founder and CEO of WomenWise.com, is a pioneer in the area of women's electronic communications in countries where mobile phones are the most common form of communication. These markets have been more accepting of games on cell phones. "People in those markets have more readily accepted mobile phones as a way of communications, especially in the way of text messaging," said Huurre. "Games and entertainment has been an easy transition and extension of the technology."

"One of the more popular games is meeting people via mobile phones not only in the form of 'online dating,' but just in meeting friends. And it's those games that form community that tend to be inviting and engaging to women."

Huurre also states that while entertainment on cell phones is becoming more acceptable, it seems that the same problems that plague the computer game industry are popping up in the wireless entertainment industry. "The developers are predominately male," says Huurre. "That's all well and good. However, just as in the traditional games industry, they are creating games *they* want to play" [Huurre03].

Nowhere is this more obvious than in the J2ME port of the classic *Prince of Persia* by Gameloft. Unlike the original *Prince of Persia* series, where the Prince is out to save his beloved Princess from the Vizier, in *Prince of Persia, Harem Adventures* he is out to save the Sultan's wives who have been kidnapped by the Vizier in order to carry out experiments on abstinence [Sundgot03]. When the Prince rescues the women, the player is rewarded with pictures of them, under which are captions such as, "I'll introduce you to Persia and its carnal delights." Huurre believes that if the developers can avoid developing games that actively drive away the female players, then the market is a natural niche for female game players. "I think there will be a fantastic future for the mobile games industry to capture the attention of the female market just because of the technology itself," says Huurre. "We know how the female and casual gamer likes quick rewards and shorter periods of time play. Just think of how many of us will be playing on subways, waiting in lines, being 'soccer moms' and the like. We can have our quick game fixes and time wasters when needed" [Huurre03].

Huurre believes that the wireless entertainment market has amazing potential for the female audience. "The key word in all of the innovations we'll hopefully see is 'entertainment,'" she says. "And that may well include our thirst for learning, social satisfaction, the ability to communicate, and nurture, as we do everyday. Entertainment will be a part of our world at our fingertips, 'on call.'"

Between online worlds and wireless communications, the opportunity for designers to reach out beyond the traditional market is immense. However, to do so, designers must keep several things in mind. They must continue to develop reward systems for nontraditional gameplay styles, they must explore genres outside of science fiction and fantasy, and they must consciously work to develop concepts that are not necessarily male specific in content.

■ **AN INTERVIEW WITH SANDRA POWERS, LEAD PROGRAMMER ON *ASHERON'S (AC) CALL* LIVE TEAM**

Sandra Powers didn't come to computer game programming via the normal ways. She didn't play games as a kid, nor did she spend all her free time on the computers in the school library. In college, she got one bachelor's degree in mathematics and then a second in anthropology. "But I didn't know what I wanted to do beyond that," she said.

The summer after she got her bachelor's in anthropology, she was house sitting for her mother, and to fill her time, she began playing Major MUD on a local BBS. "I started messing around with automated macro scripts and ended up doing more of that than I was actually playing," Powers said. "I really enjoyed the thinking that went into creating a script. You had to start out with a clear goal and build the behaviors of the script toward that goal very logically. You had to think of all the possibilities, graph out all the branches of logic, plan for each contingency—it was fun."

Her boyfriend recommended that she look into some programming classes. She did, and enjoyed them so much that she

(continued)

(continued)

continued on to get a third bachelor's degree in computer science. "I made the school's programming team and competed in the regional and national levels of the ACM International Collegiate Programming Contest," she said. "I was the only female on the team at that point, although there had been several others in the past. I wasn't really thinking of games then. I was thinking of getting a reliable, good-paying job. . . ."

With her programming degree completed, Powers and four friends applied to Turbine as programmers. Of the five, three were hired. Powers quickly moved up the ranks to serve as lead programmer on the *Asheron's Call (AC)* Live Team.

The major gender-related issue Powers has consistently had to deal with in the game industry is people not believing she is actually a programmer. But she's been comfortable at Turbine, where she says there have always been females in positions of leadership. "Katie Finin was my lead when I was hired, and the lead designer when I joined the *AC* Live Team was Kim Payson," says Powers. "Both of them are still leads at Turbine, but on different projects these days."

Overall, Powers believes that one of the powerful attractions of the online game world is its flexibility. There's something there for everyone. "Here is a persistent world to explore and make your own. It's entirely consensual; you can take it or leave it, and you have a much higher degree of control over your experiences here than you do in real life. You can pretend to be someone else— generally someone more powerful, or sexy, or competent, or socially adept than you feel you normally are. And the pseudo-anonymity of the online world let's you experiment with these roles in relative safety" [Powers03].

REFERENCES

[ACDiscussions03] Re: QoTD—How Many Females PK? on AC Discussions' electronic bulletin board, February, 2002; available online at *http://forums.warcry.com/read.php?f=52&i =135269&t=135260#135269.*

[Garvey90] Garvey, Catherine, *PLAY*, Harvard University Press, Cambridge, Massachusetts, 1990.

[Globe02] "The Globe and Mail, Will Sims Online ride to the top?" *Globe and Mail*, December, 2002, available online at *http://www.globetechnology.com/servlet/ArticleNews/tech/RTGAM/ 20021216/gtsims/Technology/techBN/.*

[Huurre03] Huurre, Anne-Marie, on females/mobile games, e-mail to author; June 6, 2003.

[NSB02] National Science Board, *Science and Engineering Indicators— 2002*, National Science Foundation, Arlington, Virginia, 2002.

[Powers03] Powers, Sandra, interview questions e-mailed to author; February 12, 2003.

[Sundgot03] Sundgot, Jorgen, "Prince of Persia for Series 60," *Infosync World*, February 2003, available online at *http://www.infosync.no/news/2002/n/3142.html.*

[WIGD02] Women in Game Development mailing list, re: tutorials, February 2002, *http://www.igda.org/women.*

[Yee03] Yee, Nicholas, "Ethnography of Online Weddings," *The Daedalus Project;* January 1, 2003, available online at *http://www.nickyee.com/daedalus/archives/000467.php.*

CHAPTER 10

THE DESIGN DOCUMENT—
A CASE STUDY

OPS COMMANDER:
ALEXANDRA BLUE

MISSION TARGET:
RESCUE TEAM LEADER

A designer was cleaning out his file cabinet when he came across a series of e-mails from his first job in the game industry in 1992. He had written them to his producer in an effort to convince him of the wisdom of using a design document when developing their next title. The producer's response was not encouraging.

It's hard to believe that not too long ago, design teams worked without written design documents or specifications of any kind. Products started with a producer's vision, and then details were directed by that person on a day-to-day basis. More often than not, however, this was an ineffective way to run a project and was one of the causes for titles being late and incredibly over budget.

Today, the majority of publishers would not consider moving forward on a project that didn't have some sort of design specifications laid out before production begins. The design document is the heart and soul of the project. It keeps the vision clearly in sight and, if used properly, helps to keep the team on schedule and on track [Michael03].

The design document is where the very first design decisions are made, and thus it is where the tone of the title is first set. It is because of this that the design document is where developers must begin to consciously build a game's roadmap with the greatest potential for broad market appeal.

10.1 PARTS OF A DESIGN DOCUMENT

Each part of the game design document offers opportunities for a designer to maximize the audience potential. By paying attention to broad ideas, content specifics, and even the language in each section, the designer can have a major influence on the overall success of a product.

While there are many different types of design documents, and each publisher has their own preferred style, a design document usually can be divided into three parts: the introduction and product overview, the gameplay overview and sample gameplay, and the technical overview.

The introduction and product overview are the first contact a potential publisher has with a title. It is usually short, has a 'teaser,' and reads like text that would appear on the back of the product box. Often, the product overview will also contain information about the game's team, including credentials and brief biographies of team members, in order to build the publisher's confidence in the team.

The gameplay overview and sample gameplay is where the designer can get into the nuts and bolts of the game design. This section usually starts with a general overview of how the designer envisions the game being played and then breaks the game into specific parts. As each section is broken into more and more detail, specific tasks are outlined, time lines and milestones are added, and this section then becomes the schedule and blueprint for the project.

The technical overview doesn't have quite as much to do with the specifics of the game design; and therefore, it won't be discussed in detail here. This is not to say that the technology outline is not important or is separate from design. Actually, it is one of the most important parts—it is what brings the design to life. If the technology doesn't support the design features that the developer wants in the title, then the title will not be possible to produce. Therefore, it is important to develop or find technology that is flexible, modular, and easily adapted to various designs. The technology overview addresses how the available technology will support the design.

10.2   SAMPLE DESIGN DOCUMENT AND REVISIONS

By looking at each of these parts of the design document a little closer, the designer can begin to see the overall effect of the document on the title. As an example, we will look at a fictional design document for a role-playing game about King Arthur and the Knights of the Round Table. We will examine the original design document and then look at ways to increase the title's audience by adjusting the tone and concepts without harming the title's integrity.

10.3 PRODUCT OVERVIEW

The product overview gives a general outline of the type of title the team is developing. It acknowledges the title's genre and specific type of game. It also talks about the team members and leadership, and comments on the company that is producing the title. The information given about the actual gameplay is short and usually reveals just enough of a 'hook' to interest the readers.

Original Game Overview

Great Games, Inc. presents *The Adventures of the Knights of the Round Table,* a role-playing game based on the legends of King Arthur. The player selects any of the four knights seated at King Arthur's Round Table, and then, in the role of that knight, as he rides off to adventure in the exciting world of medieval England. He will battle mythical beasts, rescue damsels in distress, and encounter other figures of legend such, as Merlin the Magician and the Lady of the Lake. Ultimately, he will gain pieces to a map that shows the way to that most elusive trophy, the Holy Grail. When he solves the knight's quest, he returns triumphant to the Round Table and can then select another of King Arthur's knights, take up his sword again, and tackle new challenges and adventures!

(continued)

(continued)

Great Games, Inc. was founded in 2000 when Joe Designer and Sam Programmer left Mega Corporation to pursue their first love, role-playing/adventure games. After a successful string of hit sports titles at Mega Corporation, they began to miss the genre that brought them to games in the first place. Together, they have gathered a team that includes the best names in computer game development today, and they strive for a role-playing experience that will make the player feel like he's really there.

Initially, this sounds like a fine concept—knights in shining armor, the Round Table; what could be a better subject for a game? There is, however, one glaring problem with this title. That is, there are no Arthurian legends about female knights. The majority of females in these tales are usually damsels in distress, evil and conniving witches, or the perfect and chaste objects of a knight's courtly love. Thus, there is little to no chance to offer a female avatar. Perhaps one of the four knights could be made female and adventures developed for her, but this would relegate the female players to less than half of the entire game. A player certainly isn't going to be willing to spend money on a game that they can only enjoy one-fourth of! Also, by making only one or two of the knights female, the designers are faced with the 'token female' problem, mentioned in earlier chapters. How, then, could this title be adjusted to accommodate female players?

In order to start broadening the market for this title, the designers need to stand back and look at the big picture. What is the intended gaming experience? In this case, they want the player to experience the world of King Arthur first-hand through the adventures of the knights. They also want the players to be able to play in short 'bites' and achieve a feeling of success during that time, yet be involved in an intriguing story line that will bring them back again.

However, the designers don't want to limit this play experience to males only. Perhaps, then, instead of assuming the role of four different knights, the players assume their own roles and through it attempt to locate the Holy Grail, return Camelot to its former glory, and be knighted as a member of the Round Table. During this adventure, the player will encounter the four knights and assist them on their individual quests. Each of these encounters provides something that moves the player closer to their final goal.

It is interesting to note that all through the original game overview section, the designers repeatedly refer to the player as "he." English scholars will argue that in the English language, there is no gender-inclusive form, and that "man" and "he" should be construed to mean both genders. However, when taken in light of the previously discussed study that showed developers will develop for a male audience unless specifically instructed otherwise [Huff87], then the importance of the language used in the design document becomes clear. If the designers want to truly design a gender-inclusive game, then they need to keep gender foremost in their minds by using gender-inclusive language from the very beginning.

Revised Game Overview

Great Games, Inc. presents *The Adventures of the Knights of the Round Table,* a role-playing game based on the legends of King Arthur. The Holy Grail is lost, and Camelot has fallen to ruin. The player begins their journey to become a knight and restore the

(continued)

(continued)

Round Table to its former glory. Riding off to adventure in the exciting world of Medieval England, the player encounters four of King Arthur's knights, each ensnared in their own quests. Each encounter will present new challenges and adventures as the player battles mythical beasts, finds solutions to ancient puzzles, and encounters other figures of legend, such as Merlin the Magician and the Lady of the Lake. In the end, the player returns triumphant to Camelot, restores the Holy Grail to its rightful place, and is made a full Knight of the Round Table!

Great Games, Inc. was founded in 2000 when Joe Designer and Sam Programmer left Mega Corporation to pursue their first love, role-playing/adventure games. After a successful string of hit sports titles at Mega Corporation, they began to miss the genre that brought them to games in the first place. Together, they have gathered together a team that includes the best names in computer game development today, and they strive for a role-playing experience that will make players feel like they are really there.

In this revised version the tone was changed to gender neutral. The game scope was broadened to allow avatar gender choice and the emphasis on the various knights the player will encounter highlights the episode nature of the game's action.

10.4 GAMEPLAY OVERVIEW

The gameplay overview begins to describe what the players will see and experience when they enter the game. It is where the designers begin to convey their vision for the title. As the title moves into production, the gameplay overview is expanded to include gameplay specifics, and it eventually becomes a schedule with specific tasks and milestones laid out.

Original Gameplay Overview

When the player first boots up *Adventures of the Knights of the Round Table,* he sees the room with the fabled Round Table. Seated there are four knights. There is one empty seat at the table, the Seige Perilous. The player is told that the Holy Grail has been taken from Camelot, and they are all trying to find it. The knight that finds the Grail will be named the Grail Knight and will be given the honored seat: the Seige Perilous. If the player clicks on a knight, he is asked if he would like to undertake that knight's adventures. If the player selects no, then he is returned to the view of the Round Table and the five knights.

When the player selects a knight to play, the knight gets up and leaves the room, and the camera follows him. The player is then smoothly segued into third-person perspective for the major game action. Each of the different knights offers a different type of gameplay to intrigue the player and keep him coming back.

Sir Gareth: This knight must fight the Green Knight, who has stolen a piece of the map to the Holy Grail. He must defeat the Green Knight's minions. Then, in a fierce sword battle, he must defeat the Green Knight himself.

Sir Gwaine: This adventure involves traversing a treacherous canyon and exploring a dangerous cave full of monsters. He will find the map piece hidden in a chest at the bottom of the caves.

(continued)

(continued)

Sir Bedivere: The player must locate and defeat the Mythical Questing Beast. This creature is hiding in a forest, which is a maze filled with deadly traps. The player must get through the maze safely and then defeat the great beast. The beast holds a piece of the map to the Holy Grail.

Sir Lancelot: Kind Pellimar's daughter, Elaine, has been kidnapped by the evil Mordred. The player must fight his way through Mordred's castle, defeat Mordred, and rescue Elaine. When she is returned to her father, he rewards the player with a piece of the map.

Finally, when the player has successfully completed the last knight's adventure, he finds himself in the room with the Round Table. He sees a knight place the Holy Grail onto the center of the table, and the player is then dubbed "The Grail Knight," and takes his seat at the Seige Perilous.

While this is certainly a noteworthy title and has many elements of traditional gameplay all through it, there are parts of the design that may serve as barriers for the non-traditional audience. The fact that there are no female avatars has been addressed; however, other elements, such as reward issues, conflict style, and emotional tie-in, also need to be addressed.

Revised Gameplay Overview

The game begins in first-person perspective with a trailing cam viewpoint, as the player finds him/herself standing outside the

(continued)

(continued)

gates of Camelot. Upon entering the city, the player finds it run down and nearly deserted. Even the fabled castle is standing open and vacant, the Round Table dirty and abandoned. From the few people left in the town, the player discovers that the Holy Grail has been taken, and until it is returned, Camelot and King Arthur will be lost. They are told there are four knights who are also looking for the Holy Grail, and, if found, those knights would possibly be able to help.

Now, instead of playing four separate knights, the players play themselves. This allows the players to choose their gender, which increases the comfort level for female players. Also, by providing one continuous character that will move through the various adventures, the designer increases the amount of emotional tie-in for the players and enables them to identify more closely with the avatar.

Revised Gameplay Continued

As the player begins searching for the four knights, they find each knight caught up in his own quest. The player must assist in the quests before the knights can help the player assemble the map to the Holy Grail and save Camelot.

Sir Gareth and the Green Knight: The player encounters Sir Gareth outside the Lair of the Green Knight. The Knight has beat him, and he is too injured to try again. He asks the player to confront the Green Knight, who has information on the Holy

(continued)

(continued)

Grail. The player enters the lair, where the Green Knight acknowledges that he does, indeed, have information about the Grail, but will only surrender it upon completion of the challenge that lays in wait within the lair. He tells the player that they may only use those items that are carried with them into the lair.

Once inside the lair, the player is met by an NPC who offers the player a magic stone that will keep them safe. The player may choose to take the stone or not. If they take the stone, they can walk through the dangerous maze, and the monsters are fairly easy to kill. If they do not take the stone, the monsters hit quite hard, and there is real danger to the player's character. Once the end of the maze is successfully reached, the Green Knight is there to greet them. If the player took the stone, the Knight teases them gently for not keeping their word, but congratulates them on discovering that one's word is not worth dying for a greater task lies ahead. If the player did not take the stone, then the Green Knight congratulates them on their success, but chides them for not realizing that one's word is not worth risking one's life when a higher calling lies ahead. The player is then given a piece of the map that shows the way to the Holy Grail. When the player exits the lair, Sir Gareth is waiting. He tells the player that they have proven their worth and should now continue the quest.

Sir Gwaine—The Canyon: Sir Gwaine is standing at the brink of a large and treacherous canyon. He tells the player that he has discovered that there is a map piece in a chest located in a cave at the bottom of the canyon. The walls of the canyon are steep,

(continued)

(continued)

and Sir Gwaine, being a large man, cannot traverse the canyon walls. The player, though, is smaller and more lightly armored. Perhaps they could retrieve the map piece. As the player picks their way down the canyon, they encounter puzzles reminiscent of *Prince of Persia* or *Super Mario*. There may be items along the way that the player can pick up and use to get down. Once at the bottom of the canyon, the player finds the cave and the chest, but it is guarded by monsters. The player has the choice to fight the monsters directly or use various other methods to get by them, such as luring them with food, playing music to lull them to sleep, or even poisoning them. In the end, when the player retrieves the map piece, they are magically transported back to the hillside where Sir Gwaine stands. He informs them that they have proven themselves brave and must therefore continue the quest.

Sir Bedivere—The Questing Beast: When the player finds Sir Bedivere, he is standing by a well. It seems he has been blinded by some magic of the Questing Beast and can no longer see. He asks the player to help him regain his sight and recover the map piece from the beast. He tells the player that the lair of the beast is in a grotto by the river bank. The player can locate the beast by either listening for snoring sounds or by following tracks on the ground. When the player arrives at the grotto, they find the beast is sleeping. The player can either find a way to sneak by the beast and avoid waking it, or the player can confront the beast head on. When the player reaches a chest in the back of the grotto, they find not only a map piece, but also a salve. The salve will restore Sir Bedivere's sight; he is grateful and asks the player to continue the quest.

(continued)

(continued)

Sir Lancelot—Elaine: The player comes across the Lady Elaine standing in a grove next to a castle. She tells the player that Sir Lancelot has been taken captive by the Lady Morgana, and she is trying to help him escape. Lady Morgana captured Sir Lancelot by taking his magic helm. Lady Elaine has managed to steal the helm back from Morgana, but now she must get it to Lancelot. She tells the player that she will deliver freshly baked bread to the castle to distract the guards while the player sneaks in and delivers the helm to Lancelot. This must be done cautiously, because the castle is filled with dangerous guards.

When the player delivers the helm to Lancelot, he tells them that he must now deal with Morgana. He gives the player the piece of the map he had found and urges them to continue the quest.

By providing the player with these small quests, the designer has met the original goal of the title—that of providing the players with game goals that can be accomplished in shorter, 'bite-size' intervals. An additional benefit to this style gives players small rewards for play, and they are encouraged to continue the game at a later time.

But the way the quests are structured has some substantial differences. In the original document, the various quests were obviously designed to highlight the various popular play styles of traditional games—the fighter, the puzzle, the 'action' style, and so on. In the new design, the styles are blurred slightly. Each quest now has at least two options for solving it. One of these is directly confrontational; the other will involve some sort of nonconfrontational solution.

The aspect of the players helping the knights adds to the emotional tie-in for the title. When the players help the knights, they are also helping themselves. And the ultimate goal of the quests not only makes the player a Knight of the Round Table, but it also brings peace and prosperity back to the people of Camelot. All of this makes the plot a mutually beneficial solution to a socially significant problem and increases the amount of emotional tie-in for the player.

Original Error Resolution

In each case, the player is given three lives in their attempt to solve the quest. When he dies, he uses a life and is sent back to the location where he died. If he fails three times, then he finds himself back at the Round Table, having lost any advancement he had made in that particular quest.

This section of the document addresses 'death' and how the game deals with errors. Essentially, the players are given three chances. But if they fail all three times, then they are punished for the error by being sent back to the beginning of that quest, with all forward progress in that particular quest lost. We know that this concept is not appealing at all to the female audience. It is important, then, to consider alternative ways to deal with player failure.

Revised Error Resolution

Should the player make a fatal mistake while attempting a quest, the screen will darken, and the player will awaken to

(continued)

(continued)

find themselves in an abbey. The abbey monks will tell the player that one of their order found them and brought them to the abbey for healing. The monks will offer the player the opportunity to pay for the services by solving a small problem or quest that involves the abbey. The player may choose to do this or not.

In this revised design, the player is not 'killed' and does not have to start over. Forward progress is not lost, but additional progress is impeded by the offer of a new quest that the player may feel obligated to solve. If the player does not wish to complete the monks' quest, then progress is impeded by the distance the players must travel in order to return to the location of the last quest on which they were working. It is also possible at this point for the players to simply try a different quest or a different approach to the current quest.

Another interesting aspect of this type of 'death' situation is that forcing the players to start over, as in the original version of the game, may cause players to exit a game in frustration. However, by providing forgiveness, the players are actually encouraged to stay in the game. And since these subquests are designed to have little to no bearing on the major story arc, then they are available for the players to solve at any time, making for increased play value and replayability.

10.5   TECHNOLOGY OVERVIEW

The technology overview has as much influence on the design as the actual gameplay specifications; however, its influence is in a much subtler way. It is important to assess if the technology will support the types of design decisions the designers have made. Flexibility, modularity, and ease of adaptation are the hallmarks of a good technology design. Without supporting technology, all the design in the world won't help a title's market share or even get it on the shelves.

The design document is the most powerful tool the designers have. Through this document, the designers conceive, develop, and deliver their concepts for the project. It is in the design document that the developers must begin to address the broad market to which they wish to appeal. Getting the specifics down on paper before production begins allows the designers to step back and take an objective view of the entire project. They can then evaluate it for game balance and cohesiveness, and they can also look at 'the big picture.'

The fictitious title presented in this chapter, while certainly a viable idea, is not a complete concept. Yet, it is possible to see that various areas were improved and expanded. By giving the players a choice in gender, emotional tie-in was increased and a barrier to female players was removed. By keeping the players in one character throughout the title, the player is allowed to experience a mutually beneficial solution to a socially significant problem, also contributing to the emotional tie-in to the game.

The conflict situations, which were originally very traditional, head-to-head style conflicts, were expanded to include other methods, such as stealth and manipulation. A plot line that was not only common, but potentially oppressive, was turned around to give the title a freshness and availability. Even the language was addressed, which helps to keep the designers focused on whom the title is targeted toward.

All of these steps work to turn the title from one with a traditional and limited market to one that has the potential to reach out beyond the usual audience, and this is due to the fact the developers began their work in the design document. Overall, a solid, well-developed design document is not only the designer's first step, but it is the strongest tool for developing a truly cross-market title.

REFERENCES

[Huff87] Huff, C. and J. Cooper, "Sex Bias in Education Software: The Effect of Designers' Stereotypes on the Software They Design," *Journal of Applied Social Psychology* (1987), Vol. 17, no. 6.

[Michael03] Michael, David, *The Indie Game Development Survival Guide*, Charles River Media, Inc., Hingham, MA, 2003.

CHAPTER 11

WOMEN IN THE GAME
INDUSTRY WORKPLACE

"GIRLS, GAMES, GORE, We've Got What You Want!" the banner screamed. Its latex-clad, huge-breasted 'space bunny' pouted seductively at the exhibit hall over the barrel of her huge gun. At the Women in Game Development committee's round-table session held at the same conference, a producer complained that his company simply couldn't figure out how to attract female candidates. The juxtaposition was poignant. On the one hand, the game industry had been for boys by boys from the very beginning, and proudly advertised itself accordingly. On the other hand, the maturing game industry is beginning to realize that to enjoy continued growth and expansion, it must diversify both its products and itself. But the reconciliation of these two attitudes is not easy, and resistance to change has been strong.

11.1   WHY DOES THIS INDUSTRY NEED WOMEN?

But why does the industry need women? So far, things have been going well with the male-centric teams. Titles are selling well, new hardware is well received, and the industry is out-grossing even the film industry. So, if it ain't broke, why fix it, right?

This would be a valid opinion were it not for the simple fact that the game industry is growing at a tremendous rate, but its market is not [Au02]. The traditional market for games is males ages 13–25. This market is a static number. There are only so many males of this demographic age group in the world at any one time. As some move out of the segment, others move in, but it's a fairly constant number. This means that the market saturation point will soon be reached. Without new markets to expand into and new audiences to tap, the game industry will eventually cut off its own growth paths. Because of this, the game industry must diversify their titles in order to reach new, untapped markets. The way to do this is to diversify the teams making the titles. Only in this way will the industry be able to begin to develop titles that expand their market to non-traditional audiences.

Starting at the 1999 Game Developers' Conference and each year since, the question has been raised of how a company can attract women and then retain them once they are hired. Various stories are told, but the theme remains the same. A company puts out an ad looking for designers and receives hundreds of resumes, but only a handful are from female applicants. Companies have found this confusing, as the game industry has always been a 'glamour industry' with far more people wanting in than there were positions to be filled. Usually, developers need only think about hiring someone, and the resumes come pouring in. But when looking for female applicants, this just isn't the case. If developers are serious about diversifying their teams, then they need to make the commitment to finding quality female applicants. This begins by examining their own companies.

11.2 EXAMINE THE COMPANY

If developers aren't getting the female applicants they would like to see, the first place to look is at their product lines. Are the products aimed solely at the traditional male market? Do they contain barriers that actively prevent females from becoming involved with the product, such as hypersexualized female avatars and themes of violence for violence's sake? If so, the developer will probably be fighting an uphill battle. Females, just like their male counterparts, want to make games that they would want to play. And they want to work for a company that makes the types of games they enjoy—whether that be FPSs, RPGs, or RTS games. Thus, if the company's titles are inherently unattractive to female players, then it is very unlikely that females will consider submitting their applications.

A title that contains barriers for females does more than just alienate the female audience. It also conveys an attitude toward women in general, whether it is true of the company or not. If the titles contain humor that is sexual in nature and demeans women, and/or if the game promotes hypersexual female avatars, then the company conveys the message that women are sexual objects. If they treat female characters this way in their titles, then it doesn't take much of a leap to assume this is also how they will treat women within their workplace. The impression that the industry as a whole feels this way about women hasn't been helped over the past few years with the increase in the number of provocative 'booth babes' and sexually-oriented themes at the various professional gatherings and conferences within the industry. All of these things say to the potential female applicant: "BOYS ONLY."

Once the developers have looked at their titles and determined whether they are conducive to attracting female applicants, they then need to look at their company culture. Are their employees open to the idea of having females on their teams? Often, upper management understands the need for diversification and may find several qualified female candidates, but the actual team she would be working with is not open to her presence. Teams that have been allowed to operate as 'boys' clubs' (e.g., team meetings at strip clubs or promoting a 'locker room' attitude) may not be open to having a female team member who would 'spoil their fun.' Or, they may only want a female member as a 'mascot' or even just as 'eye candy' for the team.

The company's attitude toward females is often apparent by simply looking at the studio's executive team. Does the studio have females in senior positions of power? The presence of women in upper management is automatically a positive sign for female applicants. Are there women in up-and-coming positions of leadership? A company needs to look at their past hiring practices. Have men and women been given equal consideration in promotions? Are women still in production positions, while men hired at the same time have all moved up the ladder? This is an important indicator of how seriously the women on the team will be taken and how they will be valued.

The physical appearance of the office is important as well. Are there centerfolds or other R-rated calendars on the walls? Is there sexually-oriented artwork on the walls or whiteboards? This can convey insensitivity toward women within that office. Likewise, the presence of pornographic magazines and books is also a potential barrier. While it is possible they may have some function as anatomy references for artists, it is unprofessional and inappropriate to leave them out in the open.

Probably the best litmus test of an office's acceptability to women is for the team members and managers to ask themselves if they would be comfortable showing their grandmothers around the studio, or if they would be comfortable having their mothers or sisters work on the teams. If the answer is no, then the developer needs to reconsider the company's attitude toward women before trying to recruit them.

If developers have looked at their companies and determined there are no barriers, they then need to look at how employment ads project the company's image. For example, a recent recruitment ad appeared in an industry publication. It featured a group of young men, dressed in black and wearing dark glasses, sitting by a pool, surrounded by bikini-clad young women. "Want this? Come work for us!" it proclaimed. Obviously, this type of ad would draw very few female job seekers. But the ads don't have to be that blatant. Recently at a game developers' conference, an employment ad for game designers was posted. It was a straightforward job description, listing responsibilities and requirements. However, down one side of the paper, there was art featuring the typical 'game girl'—large bust, bedroom eyes, and erect nipples. The employer in this case happened to be female. When this was brought to her attention, she admitted that she hadn't gotten any female applicants, but she hadn't considered that the ad itself might be part of the reason.

This attitude toward ads goes beyond job recruitment and extends to the types of ads run for the company's products. A t-shirt at a game developers' conference featured a sci-fi babe whose waist was smaller than her head and who had a very round derriere, and the low-cut neckline of her silver spandex costume revealed the cleavage of very large breasts. Her huge red lips were pursed in a semi-kiss over her upturned gun as she blew milky white smoke from its barrel. "Wanna play?" read the caption. While this company wasn't advertising for employees, it is likely that any female applicant who saw this overtly sexual T-shirt certainly would not consider working for the company that sponsored them. Nor would she consider the company in the future. In fact, in her future job search, this company would probably not even come up as a possibility.

11.3   FINDING THE FEMALE CANDIDATES

So, it's pretty clear how to 'turn off' female applicants. The question remains, how *should* a company advertise in order to attract the most female applicants? The first thing a company needs to do is clarify the fact that they do want female applicants and are committed to actively searching for them. Unlike traditional applicants, females up to now have not considered the game industry as a possible career choice. It simply isn't on their list when they begin a job search. Thus, it is up to the employer to actively seek them out and let them know they are interested in hiring women.

Because this is not the normal mindset for a game industry employer, they are often at a loss on where to start. Just like all good recruiting initiatives, it begins at the networking level. The network must be seeded and farmed in order to produce the type of candidates the employer is looking for. Employers should begin by contacting and interacting with any technology/game groups that are meeting in their areas. Local universities and colleges usually have at least one computer club and usually a gaming club or two. By supporting these groups, the employer can keep an ear to the ground on who's available and who will soon be available. This support may be as simple as providing pizza for the club's meetings or providing a speaker. But while these clubs and groups may want more female members, they do not usually have a high percentage of females. The employer needs to seek out those technical organizations that are aimed at women, such as Women in Technology and Women in Science. Often, these organizations will have student chapters in local universities and sometimes even in the high schools.

It may also be necessary to take a step back and work with the girls that will be entering these organizations. The Girl Scouts, YMCA, TWIST, and other girls' organizations all now have activities that emphasize technology. They provide a great opportunity for the game industry to step in with support, such as with meeting space, speakers, sponsorships to summer computer camp, and similar activities. None of these activities are terribly expensive, but they do provide a terrific farming network, as well as provide a very interesting demographic pool from which to pull focus group participants!

But this is long-range planning. What about employers who want female applicants now? In order to fill an immediate job opening, the employer needs to get creative in their recruiting effort. The female readership of traditional industry publications is quite small, so ads placed there are not going to be terribly effective. Instead, the industry needs to advertise in places with females who may have the skills necessary for game industry positions. Need artists? Consider the local art schools or programs in local universities or colleges. Need designers? How about checking the local English departments or creative writing labs. Screenplay writing workshops are a great place to find writers experienced with creating dialog. For level designers, a school of architecture or technical school that emphasizes CAD work might provide some interesting leads or even candidates. Schools that have a Radio, Television, and Film (RTF) department may provide candidates with many of the skills needed in production and development. And there are always job fairs and career expos aimed specifically at women, where developers will find candidates with an amazing array of skills and experience.

Another often overlooked resource is the developer's current employee pool. Developers should talk with the employees they already have, especially the female employees. They may have female friends that are interested in the industry, or they may belong to a network that the employer could tap into. By offering a referral bonus for employees who refer potential candidates that are accepted for employment, employers can encourage current employees to actively recruit for the company.

Sometimes the applicants need to see that the industry can be fun for females. The employers can help with this through the judicious use of internships. By advertising for interns in nontraditional areas, such as RTF or English departments, employers can get a higher number of female interns, and these interns can get a first-hand look at the possibilities for females in the industry. The internship program is beneficial to both the employer and the employee. For the interns, it gives them a 'trial run' in their chosen industry career choice. For the employer, it allows a 'try before you buy' option for future employees, and it also enables the company to train the future employee on a smaller budget.

11.4   SUPPORTING THE FEMALE EMPLOYEE

Now, if the employer has managed to attract a number of quality female applicants and has selected the perfect fit for their team, the problems are not over. Turnover is high in the game industry, a problem that is no different when it comes to female employees. Employers need to address issues that concern their female employees if they wish to retain them.

In October of 2002, the Women in Game Development mailing list did an informal survey on the concerns of potential female recruits in the game industry. The number-one concern was the amount of required overtime/crunch time. While this has gotten somewhat better in recent years, it is still a regular part of just about every game development timeline. While crunch time is hard on all employees, it has a particularly hard effect on female employees. Research shows that while partners are participating more in the work of maintaining the household and raising the children, the women still perform the majority of the work in the household [Consalvo03]. This results in very different attitudes toward what 'home' means.

For the males, home is primarily a place of rest and relaxation. He leaves his place of business and goes home to recharge. Perhaps he turns on the computer and plays a game to relieve stress. But for women, the home is only partially a place of rest and relaxation. It is also a place of work [Consalvo03]. She leaves her place of business and usually comes home to fix dinner for the kids and the husband, who is playing *Quake*. Then, after the meal, there is laundry to be done and rugs to be vacuumed. She'll only have a chance to relax when her housework is finished. Because kids must be fed and have clean socks to wear, any time that cuts into her 'home' time will have to be taken from the amount of leisure time she has. When her leisure time is cut into on an extended basis, the potential for burnout is very high.

With this in mind, employers need to ride herd on their design process in order to cut down on 'crunch time.' They can do this by providing training on project management for their production staff. Teaching project managers how to keep control of the schedule and budget will help them keep their teams on track and prevent the scheduling problems for which the game industry is famous.

Continuing education is a valuable tool for employee retention in areas other than project management. The computer game industry is growing and has numerous valuable conferences and seminars for developers to attend. The biggest is the annual Game Developers Conference sponsored by the International Game Developers Association (IGDA). This conference provides developers the opportunity to learn from industry veterans as well as from each other. Other conferences that are valuable are Siggraph, DICE Summit, and many others. When employers support their employees in attending conferences like this, they are sending the message that the employee is valuable to the company. This builds company loyalty, which is a large factor in preventing employee turnover.

But there are other options for education that don't entail sending employees to conferences. A great opportunity often exists within the company itself. All companies benefit from cross-training its employees. By encouraging the departments within a company to communicate and educate each other on what their tasks are, greater understanding of the process is achieved, and the development process is improved. Employers can plan brown-bag lunches where artists help the programmers spend an hour in hands-on time with the art tools. Or artists can spend an hour with programmers, learning about the basics and potentials of game engines.

Sharing knowledge within a department is also key to preventing what one developer calls, 'Bus People.' Bus People are employees who, should they be hit by a bus tomorrow, the company would be lost without. This lack of redundancy in key positions is a recipe for disaster. By promoting cross-training within the department, the employer can help reduce this risk. The programmer who is working on the combat system should spend time and share knowledge with the programmer who is working on the install. The artist working on the textures needs to understand what the character-animation artist is doing and why. This not only creates a layer of security for the employer, but it instills a feeling of value in the employees. It recognizes what they know and how valuable they are.

However, when presented with these learning situations, there may be some employees who are not comfortable asking questions in front of a large group. This is particularly true of female employees who from elementary school are conditioned to not ask questions [Kimmel00]. To help alleviate this problem, employers may wish to set up a mentoring program within the company. A senior employee would be assigned to a new hire, get acquainted with them, and help the new employee with any questions they may have. This relationship may last only a month or two, or it may last the entire time the employee is at the company. This gives employees an 'ally' in the company, and someone they can ask a specific question of without the fear of public humiliation.

11.5   SEXUAL HARASSMENT

So, the employer has made a commitment to finding quality female applicants, examined the company for potential barriers, restructured the hiring ads, supported the local Girl Scout troops, and found a group of highly qualified, enthusiastic female candidates from which they selected the ones that best fit the job description. Now everyone lives happily ever after, right? In reality, not always. Unfortunately, there can still be problems, and before they know it, employers can find themselves in the middle of a sexual harassment conflict. How does this happen, and what can employers do to head off problems like this?

First, it is important to understand what sexual harassment is. Sexual harassment is hostile or unwelcome behavior in the workplace, based on sex. Hostile means unwelcome behavior that is pervasive and persistent—that is, behavior that a reasonable person under similar circumstances finds hostile, based on their gender. What exactly that behavior is varies from state to state and even case to case [Cornell03]. "That is because harassment is in the eye of the beholder," says Connie Cornell, JD, PHR, a board-certified specialist in the area of employee relations in the state of Texas for 18 years. She has spent much of that time defending employers from sexual harassment suits.

"No one considers themselves a harasser," says Cornell. "They usually do not set out to offend someone purposefully." According to Cornell, even consent does not equate to welcoming the behavior or actions. "For instance, a young, single mother is invited out for a drink after work by her boss. Wanting to be seen as a 'team player,' she says yes. Once there, he suggests he'd like to get to know her *much* better and has rented a room. The woman, in fear for her job, says yes, and accompanies the boss upstairs. If she truly thought he was a great man and would be a wonderful father for her child, then this is fine. However, if she was actually thinking what an awful toad he was, and how she knew she'd lose her job if she said no, then she may have given consent, but the invitation certainly wasn't welcome. Consent does not equal welcome." Thus, the female may say she doesn't mind the pornographic calendars in the office, but that does not mean she welcomes their presence there. And it doesn't mean that these issues won't show up in a sexual harassment lawsuit.

When a sexual harassment suit is filed, there are essentially four parties involved in the suit: the employee, her attorney, the employer, and the employer's attorney. Of these four, it is the employer who is in the worst possible position. The former employee has nothing to lose, as she is already unemployed, and a win would only improve her condition. The employee's attorney has one of two possible outcomes: a win or a loss, and the payment arrangement will likely vary accordingly. The employer's attorneys will get paid regardless of who wins. It is the employer who comes out on the losing end, regardless of the outcome of the suit. If they win, they pay their attorney. If they lose, they pay the settlement as well as attorneys for both sides. Even if the employee chooses to settle the problem out of court, the employer must still pay the settlement fee as well as their attorney fees.

But there is another cost that employers may not have considered. The law says that once a complaint is made, the employer must take prompt and appropriate action. Often, this means terminating the individual against whom the complaint is made. If that person happens to be the lead programmer for the flagship title, this can be disastrous to not only the team, but to the company as well. If the company chooses not to terminate that person, then the probability of the complaint becoming a suit is increased [Cornell03]. Also, the company's morale suffers, and it is very likely that the accused person's performance will suffer simply from the stress of the complaint.

The irony of this is that it is often a preventable problem. Employers can go a long way toward preventing this type of situation by increasing employee awareness through training. Also, employers are required by law to have a harassment policy. This policy must define what harassment is, tell people where they can report it, and, if reported, guarantee that the situation will be investigated in a prompt manner, and appropriate action will be taken.

Finally, the policy must guarantee that the person filing the complaint will not be retaliated against. This retaliation can be as overt as spray painting obscenities on the person's car, or it can be as subtle as 'freezing out' the individual from the company culture. According to Cornell, cases in which there was retaliation against the person who filed the complaint will often be awarded the largest amount of damages by jurors.

Now, many employers might make light of a couple of explicit calendars in the programmers' cubicles or turn a blind eye to pornographic magazines in the art room. And everyone likes a good sexual joke every now and then, don't they? Certainly, off-color language is just something to be expected in a creative work environment. However, when the employee sits down with an attorney to prepare the complaint, they will bring up and document all of these issues; and when two years of working under these conditions is compressed into a three-day jury trial, the workplace will begin to look like Sodom and Gomorrah. Each inappropriate situation adds to the whole, and the sum can be greater than the total of the parts.

So, an ounce of prevention in this case is certainly worth the pound of cure. If employers will take the threat of sexual harassment complaints seriously and provide the necessary training for their employees, they can reduce the risk dramatically. And the money that would have been paid to attorneys can go to the team for bonuses instead!

11.6   BENEFITS FOR THE WHOLE

Bringing women into the game industry isn't without its problems. For employers to find qualified candidates, recruit them, and then retain them requires specific planning and consideration. Once the candidates are hired, employers must make certain benefits packages are maintained, project management techniques are taught and followed, and human resources policies are in place and supported. While these initiatives certainly attract and benefit female employees, it is interesting to note that, according to the male members of the WiGD (Women in Game Development) mailing list, it also increases the retention and loyalty of male employees. So, an employer that takes these steps in their hiring and recruiting program will find their entire employee base is happier, suffers from less burn-out, and is therefore more productive—regardless of their gender. It's a win-win situation for everyone involved!

MAXIS

In a world of companies dedicated to the traditional market, there is one company that stands out from the crowd. Maxis, a wholly owned subsidiary of Electronic Arts and developer of the phenomenal *Sims* titles, has a workforce of 230 people, of which approximately 40% are female. To what do they attribute this success with recruiting, hiring, and retaining female employees? According to Shannon Copur, associate producer and Maxis employee since 1996, it is directly related to the quality titles the company produces. "We don't produce violent, shoot-em-ups. Our titles are more family-oriented. You can put your kids in it and be okay." Copur also feels

(continued)

(continued)

that the open-endedness of the titles is a great attraction for women, as it allows individuals to play the games the way they want to—without barriers. "Our games are like a canvas. The player can paint whatever they want on it," she says. "Watercolor, oil, whatever. They are free to sculpt it as they want." [Copur03]

Virginia McArthur, game industry veteran since 1997 and producer at Maxis agrees. "The customization in the games is a big part of it. You can make [it resemble] your family, your house, and even you. It becomes *your* game." She goes on to add there are other things that attract women to Maxis. "A big part of why I came to Maxis was because of the other women." She says she found it refreshing to be interviewed by another woman and to see the number of women working there. She also says that Maxis made a conscious effort to reach a broader 'mass' market. This drove them to actively recruit, hire, and promote women into positions of authority [McArthur03].

McArthur goes on to explain that the reason Maxis is able to retain the number of women it has is because it is acutely aware of the requirements of family and home on their employees. To respond to this, they have implemented a flexible work environment, allowing employees to work from home if need be, and have worked to reduce or possibly eliminate 'crunch' time from production. They have also provided a generous time-off policy to compensate for whatever 'crunch' time might be required.

"However, this is still a tough industry to be female in," says McArthur. "It is a lot of work and requires a lot of energy, and then you still have to go home to the 'female responsibilities' of your household. It can still be tough." But Maxis has made great strides in making that double load a bit easier to handle.

REFERENCES

[Au02] Au, Wagner James, "Showdown in Cyberspace: Star Wars vs. The Sims," *Salon Magazine*, July 2002, available online at *http:// salon.com/tech/feature/2002/07/09/mmorpg/index.html*.

[Consalvo03] Consalvo, Mia, "Profiling the Female Gamer: A Look at How She Buys and Plays," Game Developers Conference, San Jose, California, March 2003.

[Copur03] Copur, Shannon, interview by author, Austin, Texas; April 21, 2003.

[Cornell03] Cornell, Connie, JD, PHR, interview by author, Austin, Texas, April 22, 2003.

[Kimmel00] Kimmel, Michael S., *The Gendered Society*, Oxford University Press, New York, 2000.

[McArthur03] McArthur, Virginia, interview by author, Austin, Texas; April 21, 2003.

CHAPTER 12

INFLUENTIAL WOMEN IN COMPUTER GAME DEVELOPMENT

12.1   ANNE WESTFALL

FREE FALL ASSOCIATES

There is a historic and now prophetic poster in computer game development, a 'rock album' style poster featuring the original developers for Electronic Arts (EA). The poster was entitled, "We See Farther." The only woman in the poster is Anne Westfall.

Westfall has been a constant figure in the game industry since 1982, when she and her husband, Jon Freeman, formed Free Fall Associates, a software development house. Free Fall Associates were the very first game developers signed by EA. Westfall also went on to spend four years as a director and the CFO for the Computer Game Developers Conference. "I wasn't even aware of computer games before I met Jon. I knew some existed on mainframes, but that's about it. I'd played *Space Invaders* at the pizza parlor, but that's as close as I came to computer games."

During the four years Westfall spent as CFO for the Computer Game Developers Association (CGDA), she also served as speaker manager for the Computer Game Developers Conference. "As speaker manager, I was responsible for solicitation and initial evaluation of topic proposals, and program arrangement. [I was also] the speaker liaison." In this role, Westfall had tremendous influence on what topics were presented to conference attendees and what information they took home with them.

Today, Westfall and her husband primarily develop games they consider to be quite gender inclusive. "We're currently doing card games based on *Triplicards*, a deck that Jon invented. Puzzle games or games with the feel of classic board games obviously appeal to both genders," she says.

However, Westfall does not believe that the concept of gender-inclusive games should be limiting to the potential subject matter for a game. "Only a small percentage of subjects might be off limits," she says. "The vast majority of suitable game topics should naturally appeal to both genders." According to Westfall, the growth of the Windows® operating system has helped the explosion in popularity of PCs in homes today. This has also had the benefit of making the computer a domain open to more than just teenage boys or hardcore gamers.

But the technology alone won't help expand the gender-inclusive market base. "The Internet, PCs in the home, and more different *kinds* of games do much more to expand the market base," Westfall says.

"And the industry has suffered from a number of setbacks," she says. "The success of game[s] that specifically exclude the female player, like *Grand Theft Auto 3*, encourages publishers to create more of the same. Game marketing tends to be unnecessarily exclusionary. Too often, it tells girls and women that games aren't for them."

"The 'girls' market' is still a niche market," Westfall adds. "But the market for games that appeal to girls as well as guys is enormous!" [Westfall02].

12.2   ROBERTA WILLIAMS

FOUNDER, SIERRA ENTERTAINMENT, INC.

In 1980, Roberta Williams sat at her kitchen table and worked out the design for a computer game called *Mystery House* for the Apple II computer. Her husband, Ken, did the programming for it. When it was completed, they put an ad for it in the back of *Micro Magazine* to see if it would sell. And it did. It sold so well in fact, that it served as the launch pad for one of the longest lived computer game companies today: Sierra Entertainment, Inc.

Williams was one of the first women to enter computer game development and was the first woman producer of a major selling game series. Her series *King's Quest* was groundbreaking in many ways. It was the first to have a female protagonist. It was the first (and to date only) series to have a title with two female protagonists. It pioneered many technological advances, such as being one of the first adventure titles that was not completely text driven.

Today, Williams feels that to develop gender-inclusive titles, designers need to consider entertainment criteria for both genders. "This is 'generally speaking,' though—not necessarily in specific cases," says Williams. "Generally, men like games with more action— especially violent action, games with more hand-eye coordination, and games with lots and lots of strategy. Women tend to like games with more story, more character development, and more interaction with characters—games with solving puzzles, games involving the brain rather than the hand, games with a more social aspect. And surprisingly, with hand-eye coordination games, women seem to like those types which have 'gathering' aspects to them, a good example being *Tetris*" [Wright00].

12.3   BRENDA LAUREL

CONSULTANT, SPEAKER, WRITER

In 1975, Brenda Laurel was working on her Ph.D. in theatre at Ohio State University. She was visiting a friend who worked at the Battelle Memorial Institute in Columbus, Ohio, when she saw her first computer. It was displaying pictures from space, and it totally captivated her. When her friend left his job at Battelle to start a 'little home-computer company,' he asked her to help him by doing animated fairy tales. Thus, Laurel took her first step into an industry in which she would later come to have a major influence.

She spent the next years exploring her ideas about virtual reality, theatre, and games. She spent time at such industry giants as Atari,

Activision, and Apple during their formative years, and had an influence in their direction and development.

At this time, the computer game industry simply did not believe that girls played computer games. In 1992, Laurel began to focus her attention on the problem of gender and technology, and went to work as one of the founding researchers with Interval Research.

In 1996, two events occurred that would have a profound effect on how the games industry would look at the girls market in the future. It was the year *Barbie Fashion Designer* was released, and it was the year Laurel stepped off to cofound Purple Moon, one of the very first companies dedicated specifically to developing titles for girls.

Laurel firmly believes that her time with Purple Moon and the eight CD-ROM titles she produced while there are some of her best accomplishments. "I think we made a positive difference in the world," Laurel says. "I am very proud of the work we did for girls" [Lynch].

Today, Laurel continues to support the viability of the girls' market. "It's viable in movies, TV, books, clothing, accessories—why in the world would it not be viable in computer games?" she asks. To this, Laurel believes that games like *The Sims Online* and *Ultima Online* have made tremendous inroads into the gender-inclusive market. She believes these kinds of games provide multiplayer role-playing experiences that allow for different styles of interaction, status-building, and affiliation. She would aim a game today at the teen audience, as well.

However, the balance within a gender-inclusive game may be tricky. "The Games that are typically most attractive to male players involve fast action, violence, military metaphors, etc. Females tend to be much more interested in character and story, regardless of narrative context." Laurel believes these differences are ripe for development today. "Genres, such as romance and mystery, that are typically female favorites in the world of books are basically untapped as of now." With a smile she adds, "and if anyone wants to know how to do that, tell 'em to call me" [Laurel02]!

12.4   LAURA FRYER

DIRECTOR OF XBOX TECHNOLOGIES, MICROSOFT

Laura Fryer grew up in Colorado horse country. Once a week or so, her family would pop popcorn and pull out the board games. In her teenage years, she and her brother began playing paper games, including *Dungeons and Dragons*. Later, when she was taking a basic C programming course, she discovered computer games. Today, she still loves to game with her family and often takes time off work when her brother comes to visit, just so they can spend as much time gaming together as possible, "with occasional breaks for frozen burritos."

Fryer started at Microsoft, supporting their games and multimedia titles. From there, she moved on to become a producer and was one of the first members of the Microsoft Games Studios. In that role, she was recognized as one of their most prolific producers, publishing six titles in five years.

While she was there, she recognized the opportunity that online gaming presented for Microsoft. She produced their first online title, a MMP game called *Fighter Ace 1.0*. She was instrumental in the development of The Zone, Microsoft's online game portal and the most successful of all gaming destinations.

In her current role as Director of the Xbox Advanced Technology Group (ATG), Fryer plays a key role in determining the direction of gaming in the highly competitive world of console technologies. When asked about developing broad-market games, Fryer responds that games like *The Sims* and *Zoo Tycoon* were certainly the type[s] that she would develop. "Ideally, the game would be easy to get into, but hard to master," she says, "[It] would reward a wide variety of play styles and would feature a rich and surprising world." She believes that broad-market games in an online environment are the key to market success. "The television is the major competitor for online games. It's very easy to turn on the TV and sit there for the entire night's entertainment. Online can deliver game content more frequently and will give games a chance to keep their audience more invested."

However, game developers today have to be careful not to fall into a technology trap, Fryer warns. "Game developers spend a bunch of time trying to make their game look competitive from a graphics standpoint and end up ignoring the actual game play of the product. In many cases, they end up spending all of their time working on the technology, and they don't leave any time for the designers and artists to iterate the content and to take full advantage of the technology. There are a lot of visually appealing games out there that aren't fun. . . ."

But if developers take the time to think about their design, then Fryer believes that the female market is a strong, viable market sector that is becoming more lucrative for the game industry. She believes that as girls today are brought up with the computer as part of their everyday lives, they will be more likely to play games on the computer. "My six-year-old niece . . . has no qualms about asking her mom to log on to the Internet so that they can shop for something. When she's 21, paying for things online and playing games is going to be the norm, rather than the exception" [Fryer02].

12.5   JANE JENSON

WRITER/DESIGNER

As an engineer for Hewlett Packard, Jane Jenson was working on a fiction novel in her spare time when she came across the computer game, *King's Quest IV*. She was fascinated by the idea of blending story and technology, so she contacted Sierra Entertainment, Inc., makers of *King's Quest*. A year later, she was hired as a writer and designer.

As the producer of the blockbuster *Gabriel Knight* game series, Jenson has made her mark as a producer who works hard to build computer games that contain deep stories and entirely addicting gameplay. "I have always been fascinated with the idea of creating a fictional world that others could explore," she says.

But the trend of today's games has her concerned. "I feel that the technology race in games that occurs on PCs does limit the audience, because only a small number of hardcore gamers actually have all the latest and greatest processor speeds, accessories, etc. With that kind of scenario, you are never going to draw in new gamers." Jenson also believes the industry has narrowed its own profit potential by limiting their products to a young male mentality. "I believe *The Sims* is selling mostly to 12–18-year-old girls, which is amazing given their sales figures. The girls' market and the mature women's market are both areas with huge potential[s] that are currently being completely ignored by the game industry."

To overcome this sort of problem, Jenson believes the industry must take into consideration the growth of causal gaming online. "Sites like zone.com have brought a lot of the general population into 'gaming' that have never, and probably would never buy games in a video game store." According to Jenson, the demographics of online gaming are much closer to the actual population demographics than the audience for either PC or console titles.

Because of this, Jenson believes that the game industry can learn a lot from modern entertainment media. By looking at the popular entertainment and finding those that have a strong, cross-gender appeal, the industry can begin to clue in on what works and what doesn't. "For instance," she says, "shows like *Buffy the Vampire*

Slayer or *X-Files* have a strong cross-gender audience. I think a good combination of a scary or mysterious plot line and a strong character relationship can appeal to both men and women."

However, Jenson does caution against adding strongly stereotypical elements into games that are intended to be gender inclusive. "I would not try to put in elements that just appeal to women, such as super heavy/syrupy romance. . . . On the other hand, I wouldn't put in a lot of action to try to draw men to a women's game. You'll end up losing both audiences." Because of this, Jenson feels that the idea of gender-inclusive games does limit the subject matter for computer games slightly. "Not too many women would enjoy playing a game where the main character is a macho, cigar-smoking sergeant, and the setting is a war zone," she says. "In the same vein, not many guys would be caught dead playing a 12-year-old girl with pigtails in a dollhouse." However, aside from obvious stereotypes, Jenson believes that gender-inclusive games can be about almost any subject.

For the future of gaming, Jenson feels that the trend toward developing titles specifically aimed at the young male market is slowing down. The arrival of online gaming and the popularity of titles like *The Sims* is certainly helping the industry to see the value in developing gender-inclusive titles [Jenson02].

12.6   ELLEN GUON BEEMAN

PROJECT MANAGER, MONOLITH PRODUCTIONS

As project manager for the *Wing Commander* series of games, Ellen Guon Beeman was responsible for some of the first titles to interweave RPG play style into a flight sim game. During this time, the *Wing Commander* team also pioneered the use of digital audio in computer games. "Two weeks after *Wing Commander II* shipped, you couldn't buy a digital audio sound card in any store in the United State. They were completely sold out," says Beeman. "Someone from Creative Labs thanked us once for building their market for them!"

Beeman is known as an innovator and driver in the computer game industry, having done everything from produce for major publishers to running her own development house. She started playing computer games as a child when her father, an engineer, brought different machines into the house. "We had an Atari and TRS-80," she says. "I started learning to program on the TRS-80 once I got into high school."

But computer games were not where she intended to go. "I was working as a producer in a small music studio when I met Christy Marx," says Beeman. "She helped me break in to television writing. My first sale was to her show, *JEM*, an animated series about an all-girl glamour rock group." When Christy Marx went on to take a design job with Sierra Entertainment, Inc., she took Ellen Beeman's resume in. Beeman's television writing experience quickly won her a project manager's slot there. "So I owe a great debt to Christy for helping me break into not one, but two industries!"

As for the market today for gender-inclusive titles, Beeman does not believe that games should be marketed as 'male,' 'female,' or 'gender-inclusive.' She believes that a game that appeals to both genders comes out of solid, thoughtful game design. "It's more a case of deliberately not limiting your market, as opposed to expanding it," she says.

She does feel there are some exceptions to this, though. She doesn't believe first-person shooters or flight sims are inherently friendly to females. "I like them," she says with a laugh, "but I recognize that I'm a mutant, really."

As for developing titles specifically for girls, Beeman feels the potential is there, but that the girls game market was hurt by the release of many poorly performing games. "The reality is that young women are becoming more and more comfortable with technology, especially online, [such as] e-mail and instant messages," she says, "so there is a technologically literate, potential game market there *if* more companies will be willing to address it. My guess is that the 'killer game app' for girls will be a wireless/online application that's a game heavily disguised as an online community" [Beeman02].

12.7 NICKY ROBINSON

DIRECTOR OF TECHNOLOGIES, STUNT PUPPY ENTERTAINMENT

In 1983, Nicky Robinson had finished her degree from University of California (UC), Santa Cruz in biochemistry, and she had her acceptance letter to UC Davis Veterinary school in hand. It was the summer before she was to start when her husband got a job porting a little computer game called *Picnic Paranoia* from the Atari to the Commodore 64. "It was a cute game," says Robinson. "You had to defend your picnic lunch from ants, spiders, and wasps."

"This was in the days when programmers were required to do it all, including the art," says Robinson. "My [former] husband was a terrible artist. I wasn't much better, but I was better than him, so I help[ed] out by making spiders for him. But I wanted to see them moving [and] see them animate. He was still working on the ants and I got impatient, so I found a book about basic Assembly programming and went to work. Within a short time, I had them animating, and I was hooked. At the end of the summer, I called UC Davis and told them, 'Thank you, but no thank you!'"

Thus began the programming career of the woman who has been called the "Father of the Game Developers Conference." According to Robinson, she and Chris Crawford where chatting one day about the lack of communication within the game industry. She told him what the industry needed was a really good, informative seminar or conference. This planted the seed in Crawford's mind, which went on to germinate and become the Computer Game Developers Conference. "Chris likes to say that I planted the seed, so I'm the father of the conference. He brought it to life, so he's the mother," Robinson says with a laugh. Robinson went on to serve several years on the board of directors of the CGDA and worked as volunteer coordinator at many of the early Computer Game Developers Conferences.

Robinson believes that if today's developers want to broaden their markets, they need to concentrate on developing depth in their designs, but should stay away from gender stereotypes. "I don't think a game that attracts women has to be all touchy-feely and *Kum Ba Yah,* but there needs to be depth to the gameplay," says Robinson. "For instance, I love the idea of a pirate game. I play all the pirate games that come out. I think the idea of shooting at other ships is good and belongs in a pirate games. But there should be something more, something like, I'm also searching for pieces of a map so I can find a lost family, too."

"Girls and boys don't like all the same thing. But they do have areas that overlap," she says. "I think developers need to find that area. *The Sims* is a great example. It's a 'gamers game' in that you have to be the type that wants to play a game for extended time periods. On the other hand, it's not a gamer's game, as it appeals to both genders. Really a smart design!" says Robinson. "I wouldn't do a shooting game, and I wouldn't do a game that was strictly relationship based. Those are both too stereotypical and would drive part of the audience away."

"Overall, " says Robinson, "I'd rather do games that were for both boys and girls. It's simply more fun to try to think of what would be fun for both. And it's certainly more profitable!" [Robinson02].

REFERENCES

[Beeman02] Beeman, Ellen Guon, interview questions e-mailed to Sheri Graner Ray; November 12, 2002.

[Fryer02] Fryer, Laura, interview questions e-mailed to Sheri Graner Ray; November 6, 2002.

[Jenson02] Jenson, Jane, interview questions e-mailed to Sheri Graner Ray; November 12, 2002.

[Laurel02] Laurel, Brenda, interview questions e-mailed to Sheri Graner Ray; November 12, 2002.

[Lynch] Lynch, Diane, "Purple Moon Setting," available online at *http://www.abcnews.go.com/sections/tech/WiredWomen/ wiredwomen990309.html*.

[Robinson02] Robinson, Nicky, interview questions e-mailed to Sheri Graner Ray; November 12, 2002.

[Westfall02] Westfall, Anne, interview questions e-mailed to Sheri Graner Ray; November 12, 2002.

[Wright00] Wright, K., Ph.D. and Abby Marold, Game Goddess Roberta Williams (2000), WomenGamers.com, available online at *http://www.womengamers.com/interviews/roberta.html*.

CHAPTER 13

BUT WHAT IF THE PLAYER IS FEMALE?

OPS COMMANDER:
ALEXANDRA BLUE

MISSION TARGET:
RESCUE TEAM LEADER

W hen *Barbie Fashion Designer* (Mattel) showed up on the retail computer game shelves in 1996, it blew away the largest misconception in the game development industry—that girls don't play computer games. The financial success of *Barbie®* titles soon had publishers scrambling to develop something that would capture a piece of this exciting, new, and lucrative market.

Unfortunately, this did not result in better-designed games or an honest evaluation of what females wanted in computer entertainment. With the exception of a few intrepid developers, it resulted in an industry that simply tried to recreate the *Barbie* title numbers by cloning these games again and again. Thus, the girls' market came to be defined not so much as a market, but as a genre of shopping, make-up, and fashion games for girls ages 6–10—a market which was then quickly saturated.

When these titles didn't succeed like their progenitor, the industry decided the market was not as lucrative as they thought. So they went back to developing titles for the traditional market of males, ages 13–25.

What the industry overlooks is that this short-sightedness has left a huge hole in the market. Girls that play *Barbie* games do grow up. With no titles for them to graduate to, they simply spend their money elsewhere. It doesn't have to be this way.

By looking at the differences in male and female entertainment criteria, and applying this information to the titles the industry is developing, it is possible to remove the barriers that prevent the female market from accessing those titles. And it is possible to do this without putting *Doom* into a pink box or making games about fuzzy kittens.

It can be done by looking at some of the basic foundations of game design and recognizing that males and females may deal with game basics in very different ways. From the first contact with a title, their differences in approach can be seen.

The avatar is the first thing a player comes in contact with, usually on the package cover. How the players experience the game through their avatars can be greatly enhanced with an understanding of the importance of avatar presentation and representation. When the female avatar is hypersexualized, it is highly likely the female player won't even consider the title. This 'eye candy' may be pleasing for male players, but they are a barrier for female players.

Also, providing avatars that are gender stereotyped in their roles in the game, or are limited in their scope, serves to push away the female audience. Likewise, if designers know that sexually-oriented humor that contains 'put-downs' of females will cause female players to walk away, they can avoid inadvertently adding content that will drive away a sizeable portion of their sales audience.

Differences in learning styles can affect whether or not a player actually plays the game when they first come in contact with the tutorial and, if it is a demo, whether the player actually buys it. Females want a modeling style of learning, whereas males prefer a more explorative method. If designers keep this in mind, they can work to develop tutorial styles that will best benefit both genders and make game tutorials seamless and natural for all players; the player is encouraged to enter the game, and their level of enjoyment is increased [Gottfried86].

Even the basic concept of the game can be a barrier for some players. The concept of conflict usually serves as the basic premise for any game title. If it is apparent from the game description that the resolution of the conflict is only going to be handled in the traditionally male manner—that is, a confrontational resolution—then this will dissuade those players that would normally choose other resolution styles, such as negotiation or compromise. With the knowledge of how each gender handles conflict, designers can build resolutions into their games that complement both styles and appeal to both audiences.

The stimuli designers use to capture their audience and keep their attention can have an effect on which markets find the title engrossing as well. Males are physically stimulated by visual input. Females may enjoy visual stimulus, however, they do not have a physical response to it. Their response comes from emotional or tactile input. So games that rely on fast movement and visual special effects may not capture the female market as well as they do the male market. By understanding this difference, designers can balance the stimuli they are using for their game and attract and keep a greater percentage of their players.

When the players have actually entered the game, how they are rewarded for their successes can either reinforce a positive game experience or it can demotivate the players. While males prefer punishment for error in a game, females prefer forgiveness. Punishment for errors is the classic method by which games are resolved. The player is given a limited number of 'lives' and has only so many 'chances' to succeed. If they do not succeed, then they are usually returned to the beginning of the level, and all progress on that level is lost.

Forgiveness for error means the loss is not permanent. Instead, it is a temporary loss, or progress toward the final goal is slowed; but it can be regained quickly, normal gameplay resumed, progress can be continued. There is no 'dying' and starting over.

Often for females, the reward of 'winning' or achieving a high level is simply not enough reason to play a game. They want to find a solution that is mutually beneficial and socially significant. They want to accomplish something, rather than 'win.' By understanding this, designers can adapt their reward system and their victory conditions to better accommodate different player expectations.

Even how males and females use computers is basically very different. Males wish to conquer the machine. They want to use it as an expression of physical power. Females want to work with the machine. They want to use it to expand their communications powers. However, because of the limited amount of cross-gender entertainment software, females have come to view computers not so much as an entertainment medium, but as a communications and productivity tool instead [Turkle98].

Why is it important for females to play games? There are two reasons. One reason is ideological, and the other is economic.

Ideologically, it is vitally important that girls play and enjoy computer games because it increases their comfort level with technology, and this is essential for them to maintain economic parity with males in today's society. If girls are not allowed to have fun with technology today, we cannot expect them to excel with technology tomorrow.

However, the more economic reason is that the game industry must expand to other markets if it wishes to sustain growth. There are only so many males age 13–25 in the world at any given time. If no other audiences are farmed, then the game industry will outgrow its market, resulting in loss of revenue and ultimately a contraction of the industry. Add to that the fact that females control an ever-growing percentage of the disposable income, then it makes sense to appeal to them if this industry wants 'a piece of the action.' However, to do this, designers must be willing to look at play patterns and models that are not necessarily their own. It is going to take producers/publishers who are willing to diversify their workforces by making a concerted effort to seek out qualified female candidates. It also means that those women who are already in the industry must be willing to serve as role models and mentors for the women who want to break into the industry. And overall, it's going to take an industry that is willing to step back, take a look at their titles, and ask themselves, "But what if the player is female?"

REFERENCES

[Gottfried86] Gottfried, Allen W. and Catherine Caldwell Brown, *Play Interactions, The Contribution of Play Materials and Parental Involvement to Children's Development,* Lexington Books, Mississippi, 1986.

[Turkle98] Turkle, Sherry, "Computational Reticence; Why Women Fear the Intimate Machine," In C. Kramare (ed), *Technology and Women's Voices,* New York: Routledge & Kegan Paul.

INDEX

A

action/adventure games, 88
Age of Empires, 38
American Laser Games, 86
Anarchy Online, 102, 103, 119
arcade industry
  environment of, 57–58, 59
  patronage of, 19, 58
Archer, Cate, 34–35
Asheron's Call, 10, 105
Asteroids, 18, 94
attitudes, gender-based and
  technology, 6, 11–14
attract loops, 70
avatars. *See also* characters
  customization of, 10, 105–106
  evolution of, 94–95
  female, history of, 27–28
  gender and race, choosing, 27
  plot lines of, 29
  power stratification and
    gender, 96
  representation of, 102–105, 181

B

backstory and game design, 61–64
Barbie Fashion Designer, 31,
  169, 180
Beeman, Ellen Guon, 173–175
Black and White, 59, 87–88
Broderbund Software, 23
bus people, 157

C

Carmen San Diego, 23–24
cel animation and game design, 20
characters. *See also* avatars
  balanced female, 23
  classes, token, 100–101
  death of, 90, 182
  development of, 20–21
  female speaking role, 19
  representations, early, 18–21
Cinematronics, 20
Classic Gaming Web site, 19
communication styles, electronic
  females, 72
  game design, 79–80
  males, 73
competition
  direct defined, 42
  direct *vs.* indirect, 45
  indirect and online games, 120
computers
  and gender socialization,
    3–5, 8–9
  use of, 182–183
conflict
  and game design, 40–42
  situations, subjects of, 38–40
conflict resolution
  gender based, 43–45, 181
  history of, 43–44
  and online gaming, 120
continuing education in the
  gaming industry, 156

cooperative play and game
design, 85–88

Cornell, Connie, 158–159

Crawford, Chris, 175, 176

Croft, Lara, 31–33

D

Daedalus Project, 120

damsel in distress concept,
challenging, 21–24

design documents. *See also*
documentation

gameplay overview, 131,
135–143

parts of, 130–131, 144

product overview, 131, 132–135

technical overview, 131,
143–144

Diablo, 40, 100–101

DICE Summit, 156

documentation, 12–13, 77–78,
122–123. *See also* design
documents

Donkey Kong, 19–20

Dragon's Lair, 20–21

Duke Nukem: Land of the Babes, 63

Duke Nukem 3D, 30, 62–63, 79

Dungeon, 29

Dungeon Master, 26

E

emotional stimulation, 56–57

emotional ties and marketing,
111–112

entertainment
criteria, female, 111, 120
wireless, 60, 124–126

error response, 8, 84–85, 89

Everquest, 119

Eye of the Beholder, 26

F

Fantasy Role Playing Game (FRP),
9–10

fertility, indicators of, 102

Fighter Ace 1.0, 170

fighting games
backstory design, 62, 63
and game design, 47, 78
and hidden moves, 70

Finin, Katie, 127

flight simulators
conflict resolution, 47–48
spatial relations, 70, 74

force feedback technology, 58–59

FPS games
backstory design, 62
reward concepts, 88
spatial relations, 70, 74
territorial control scenarios,
39, 46, 47

Free Fall Associates, 166

Freeman, Jon, 166
Frogger, 19
FRP. *See* Fantasy Role Playing
    Game (FRP)
Fryer, Laura, 170–171
FTL Inc, 26
Funcom, 34

G

Gabrial Knight, 54
game defined, 40–42, 87
game design. *See also* design
    documents
    activity based, 9–11
    avatars, 94–95, 105–106
    backstory, 61–64
    Barbie Fashion Designer, 31
    and communication, 79–80
    communication styles,
        electronic, 73–74
    and conflict resolution, 46–49
    consequences, 13–14
    cooperative play and, 85–88
    documentation, 12–13, 77–78
    emotional stimuli and, 60–61
    error response, 8, 84–85, 89
    failure, consequences of, 8
    fighting games, 47, 78
    and gender considerations,
        6–8, 95
    hot spots and, 75–76

images, female, 28–29, 33,
    102–105
    influences on, 25
    intuitive interfaces, 71–72,
        122–123
    online, 119–122, 126
    and player motivation, 9,
        10–11, 84
    puzzle incorporation, 113–115
    pyramid of power, 95–100
    rewards, use of, 182
    and risk taking, 76–77
    spatial relations and, 69–70,
        74–75
    and tactile stimuli, 60
    technological advances in, 18,
        19, 25, 31
    zero-sum outcomes and, 41, 42
Game Developers Conference, 156
Gameloft, 125
games, online
    flexibility of, 118–119
    reward systems in, 119
    story in, 119–121
    wireless entertainment,
        124–126
gaming industry
    company barriers to women,
        149–152
    recruiting women, 152–155
    sexual harassment, 157–161
    supporting women, 155–157
    women in, 148–149
Garriot, Richard, 29, 118

Garvey, Catherine, 85, 123
Gauntlet, 22–23
gender differences
    communication styles,
      electronic, 72–73
    competition, 42, 45, 120
    computers and gender
      socialization, 3–5, 8–9
    conflict resolution, 43–45, 181
    emotional stimulation, 56–57
    error response, 8, 84–85, 89
    game design, 6–8, 95
    marketing, 5–6, 180
    risk taking behaviors, 70–71
    spatial relations, 68–69
    stimulation response,
      54–56, 182
    tactile stimulation, 57–60
    technology, gender-based
      attitudes, 6, 11–14
Girl Scouts, 153
Girls Preferences in Software
    Design: Insights From a Focus
    Group, 84
graphics technology advances,
    19, 25
gymnastics and competition, 45

H
Hadza culture and conflict
    resolution, 43
Her Interactive, 4, 13, 44, 48, 84

Hopson, John, 111
hot spots and game design, 75–76
Huure, Ann-Marie, 124, 125

I
ICO, 55, 56
id Software, 39
Illusion Machines, 89
images, female, 28–29, 33,
    102–105
Indian caste system and power
    structure, 98–99
interfaces, intuitive, 71–72,
    122–123
International Game Developers
    Association (IGDA), 156
internships in the gaming
    industry, 154

J
Jenson, Jane, 54, 171–173

K
Kafi, Yasmin, 7, 84–85
Kim, Scott, 110, 112, 113
King's Quest, 25, 168
King's Quest: The Princeless Bride,
    27–28
King's Quest IV, 171

L

laser-disc technology, 20
Laurel, Brenda, 4, 85, 168–170
Leather Goddesses of Phobos, 21–22
Legend of Zelda, 24
The Longest Journey, 34
Lucas Film, 24

M

Maniac Mansion, 24
marketing
    emotional ties and, 111–112
    gender based, 5–6, 180
    market research, history of,
        2, 4–5
Mastermind, 113
Maxis, 121
McKenzie and Co., 77, 114–115
Meretzky, Steve, 21, 22
Micro Magazine, 167
Midway, 18
Miller, Rand, 54
Miller, Robyn, 55
Molyneux, Peter, 59
Monolith Productions, 34
Mortal Combat II, 86
motivation. *See* player motivation
Ms. Pac-Man, 18
mutually beneficial situations
    defined, 56
Myst, 14, 54–55, 56, 57, 69–70
Mystery House, 167

N

National Science Foundation, 121
Non-Player Characters (NPC's),
    55–56
*No One Lives Forever: A Spy in
    H.A.R.M's Way*, 35
*No One Lives Forever: The
    Operative*, 34
NPC's. *See* Non-Player Characters
    (NPC's)

O

online games. *See* games, online
Origin Systems, 105, 118

P

Pac-Man, 18, 45, 94
Pajitnov, Alexey, 110, 112,
    113–114
Pandora's Box, 111
patriarchal system in society, 96–98
Phantasmagoria, 28
Picnic Paranoia, 175
player motivation
    females and violence, 84
    game design, 9, 10–11
Player-vs-player, 119, 120–121,
    123–124
Play (Garvey), 123
Pong, 18
power, pyramid of, 95–100

power and money control
   scenarios, 39–40
Powers, Susan, 120, 126–127
Prince of Persia, 25–26, 125
*Prince of Persia: Harem
   Adventures,* 125
productivity titles and
   socialization, 4–5
protagonists, female, 25–26
Purple Moon, 169
puzzles
   audience for, 112
   defined, 110–111
   types of, 113
PvP. *See* Player-vs-player
pyramid of power, 95–100

R
raster graphics, 19
Rayson, Kim, 127
Real Time Strategy (RTS), 11, 38,
   41, 47–48, 62, 88–89
rewards, use of, 88–89, 119, 182
risk taking behaviors, females *vs.*
   males, 70–71
Robinson, Nicky, 175–176
Role Playing Games (RPGs), 41,
   75, 78, 88
RPG. *See* Role Playing Games
   (RPGs)
RTS. *See* Real Time Strategy (RTS)
Ryan, April, 34

S
scenarios
   power and money control,
      39–40
   territorial control, 38–39, 46, 47
sexual harassment, 157–161
sexuality and avatar
   representation, 102–105
side-scrolling game defined, 24
Sierra, 27
Siggraph, 156
Sim series, 87, 88, 121
The Sims Online, 118–119,
   121–122
Smith, Lisa, 29, 46
socialization
   competition, gender differences
      and, 42, 45, 120
   computers and gender, 3–5,
      8–9
   images, female, 28–29, 33,
      102–105
   power, pyramid of, 95–100
   productivity titles and, 4–5
   sexuality and avatar
      representation, 102–105
solitaire, 112
spatial relations
   flight simulators, 70, 74
   FPS games, 70, 74
   game design and, 69–70, 74–75
   male *vs.* female, 68–69
StarCraft, 38

Star Wars, 48

stimulation response
    emotional, 56–57
    evolution of, 52–53
    female, 54–56, 182
    and game design, 60–61
    male, 52–54, 182
    Non-Player Characters and,
        55–56
    tactile, 57–60
    wireless entertainment, 60

story and female attraction, 120

Strategy Plus Magazine, 46

Street Fighter II, 27

Strike Commander, 39

T

tactile stimulation, 57–60

technology
    advances, 18, 19, 25, 31
    force feedback, 58–59
    gender-based attitudes, 6,
        11–14
    laser-disc, 20

territorial control scenarios,
    38–39, 46, 47

Tetris, 45, 110, 112

Thief, 76

Tomb Raider, 31–33

*Tomb Raider: Angel of
    Darkness,* 33

Tomb Raider: Cradle of Life, 33

Turbine Interactive, 120

Turkle, Sherry, 6

tutorials. *See* documentation

TWIST, 153

U

Ultima Online, 10, 105, 118

Ultima PC game series, 10, 29,
    75, 88

*Ultima Underworld: The Stygian
    Abyss,* 47

*Ultima VII Part Two: The Serpent
    Isle,* 27, 29, 46, 105

V

Vampire Diaries, 13, 89

video arcades. *See* arcade industry

W

Westfall, Anne, 166–167

Westwood Studio, 26

Williams, Roberta, 28, 167–168

Wing Commander, 39

wireless entertainment
    online games and, 124–126
    puzzles and, 113–114
    and tactile stimulation, 60

Wolfenstein 3D, 39

Women In Game Development
   mailing list, 11, 155
Women in Science, 153
Women in Technology, 153
WomenWise.com, 124

X
Xena, 104–105
Xena: Warrior Princess, 104

Y
Yee, Nicholas, 120
YMCA, 153
youth, indicators of, 102

Z
zero-sum outcomes and game
   design, 41, 42
The Zone, 170